REMARKS

ON

SOME FUNDAMENTAL QUESTIONS

IN

POLITICAL ECONOMY

REMARKS

ON

SOME FUNDAMENTAL QUESTIONS

IN

POLITICAL ECONOMY

ILLUSTRATED BY

A BRIEF INQUIRY

INTO

THE COMMERCIAL STATE OF BRITAIN

SINCE THE YEAR 1815

BY

JOHN CRAIG

[1821]

REPRINTS OF ECONOMIC CLASSICS

AUGUSTUS M. KELLEY · PUBLISHERS

NEW YORK 1970

First Edition 1821

(Edinburgh: *Printed for* Archibald Constable & Co.;
and Hurst, Robinson & Co., *London*, 1821)

Reprinted 1970 by
AUGUSTUS M. KELLEY · PUBLISHERS
REPRINTS OF ECONOMIC CLASSICS
New York New York 10001

I S B N 0 678 00684 9
L C N 70 121321

PRINTED IN THE UNITED STATES OF AMERICA
by SENTRY PRESS, NEW YORK, N. Y. 10019

REMARKS

ON

SOME FUNDAMENTAL DOCTRINES

IN

POLITICAL ECONOMY.

REMARKS

ON

SOME FUNDAMENTAL DOCTRINES

IN

POLITICAL ECONOMY;

ILLUSTRATED BY

A BRIEF INQUIRY

INTO THE

COMMERCIAL STATE OF BRITAIN,

SINCE THE YEAR 1815.

By JOHN CRAIG, Esq. F. R. S. E.

AUTHOR OF " ELEMENTS OF POLITICAL SCIENCE."

EDINBURGH:

PRINTED FOR

ARCHIBALD CONSTABLE AND CO. EDINBURGH;

AND HURST, ROBINSON, AND CO. LONDON.

1821.

INTRODUCTION.

Nᴏᴛ long after I had published *Elements of Political Science*, in which I had endeavoured to simplify some of the principles of Political Economy, and to apply them to an examination of the several taxes levied in Britain, I had the pleasure of meeting with the second edition of M. Say's Traité d'Economie Politique, in which I found many opinions analogous to my own, supported by very similar views and illustrations. In remarking this similarity, it is unnecessary to disclaim the most distant intention of ascribing those opinions of M. Say to a work with which he could not possibly be acquainted; but it may not be superfluous to guard myself against the charge of plagiarism, by declaring that I had not then, nor have I yet, seen the first edition of his excellent Treatise. It is, at the same time, some presumption of the truth of such opinions as we have both adopted, in opposition occasionally to the doctrines of Dr Smith our great master in the science, that, without the slightest connection with each other, we have been led, in many instances, by nearly the same trains of reasoning, to the same conclusions*.

* In M. Say's Lettres à M. Malthus, I observe

The seven years that have elapsed since the publication to which I have alluded, have been very fertile in writings on subjects connected with Political Economy, and have even given birth to some new systems, by which many of the received principles of that science would be subverted. It is only very lately that I have had it in my power to examine those recent publications with the attention which they require; and I confess that the

---

that his excellent Treatise has now reached a fourth edition. But as I have not met with either of the later editions, my references are always to the second. These references are much rarer than they would otherwise have been, had I not known that the Treatise is familiar to every one who takes interest in the science. I regret that the Notes written by M. Say to the French translation of M. Ricardo's work have never fallen into my hands.

result has been to confirm the opinions I had previously adopted, and to impress me with the idea, that the great fundamental doctrines of Political Economy were capable of being presented to the student in a much simpler form, than any of those in which, in this country at least, they have lately appeared.

It would be folly to deny, that I entered on the inquiry with considerable prepossessions in favour of most of Dr Smith's opinions, and not without expectation, that, in the instances in which I had found it necessary to depart from any of the doctrines of that eminent philosopher, I should be found to have merely followed out the masterly views which he had opened up in other parts of his invaluable work. Neither will I conceal, that I felt some portion of that repugnance, natural to every one who has studied a science, to discard convictions become, as it were, a portion of my mind, and to begin again the study of new principles, and, in some instances, of new meanings attached to terms, with which, in their old significations, I was familiar. Whether those feelings have made me persevere in error, it is not for me to decide; but if my adherence to my former opinions have no better foundation, the remarks, which I now venture to lay before the public, will not for an instant retard the progress of truth.

The nature of this little tract renders it impossible to avoid all appearance of controversy; but from my respect for those authors, whose conclusions I feel it impossible to adopt, I trust I am in no danger of using any expressions that can give offence; and I am conscious that, intentionally at least, I shall give no unfair representation of the doctrines which I controvert. These doctrines I should have stated in the words of their authors, had I not been aware, that there is no kind of misrepresentation more difficult to guard against, than that produced by the separation of sentences, or even paragraphs, from the observations by which they are introduced or succeeded.

Almost every opinion that we can form in Political Economy, and especially in that most important branch of it which treats of public revenue, must be influenced by the notions we have embraced of the nature of value, and of the laws which regulate wages, profit, and rent. To each of these subjects, a short chapter is dedicated in the following Treatise; and with them it would have ended, had not the state of Britain, since the termination of the late war, besides being an object of great interest in itself, afforded several tests of the truth of those fundamental doctrines on which the science has been reared.

Edinburgh, *March* 1821.

CONTENTS.

REMARKS, &c.

ON

POLITICAL ECONOMY.

CHAPTER I.

OF VALUE.

" THE word *value* (it is observed by Dr Smith*),
" has two different meanings, and sometimes ex-
" presses the utility of some particular object,
" and sometimes the power of purchasing other
" goods which the possession of that object con-
" veys. The one may be called " value in use ;"
" the other, " value in exchange." The things

---

* Wealth of Nations. Book. I. chap. 4.

" which have the greatest value in use, have fre

" quently little or no value in exchange; and,

" on the contrary, those which have the greatest

" value in exchange, have frequently little or no

" value in use. Nothing is more useful than

" water; but it will purchase scarce any thing;

" scarce any thing can be had in exchange for

" it. A diamond, on the contrary, has scarce

" any value in use; but a very great quantity of

" other goods may frequently be had in ex-

" change for it."

This distinction, at first view, seems natural and obvious; but few students, I believe, have made much progress in the science of Political Economy, without occasionally finding the doctrines to which it has given rise perplexing; and even Dr Smith himself has incurred the imputation of confounding in his reasonings those kinds of value which he had carefully distinguished in his definitions.

It may be doubted, indeed, whether the

distinction be really founded in the nature of things, or whether it be not a mere distinction in terms, calculated to perplex, if not to mislead.

There are, it is true, a few things absolutely necessary to man's being or welfare, which, from existing in quantity equal to the desires of every one, are never appropriated or exchanged. Air and light, though of the very highest necessity, being enjoyed by every person in an equal degree in the same climate, and being also incapable of appropriation, have no exchangeable value, and are never enumerated as articles of wealth. But neither have they any connection with the science of Political Economy, which endeavours, by comparison of different countries and different times, to ascertain the causes of the growth and decline of the wealth of nations. To such a science that must be entirely foreign, of which the quantity can neither be increased nor diminished by human knowledge or human exertion.

Setting aside, then, those bounties of nature with which Political Economy has no concern, it may be asserted that the wealth either of an individual or a nation consists entirely in the appropriation of commodities having value in use, and is strictly proportioned to the quantity of such commodities, and their power of yielding pleasure, safety, or some other kind of gratification. It would, indeed, be nearly a contradiction in terms to say, that what, from its conducing neither to existence nor happiness, can be no object of desire, is yet to be considered as part of our wealth; or that what yields us gratification does not, exactly in proportion to that gratification, constitute part of our riches. The diamond may appear to a philosopher a useless bawble; but independently of its intrinsic beauty, it attracts the gaze of the multitude, marks superior wealth, and flatters the vanity of its possessor; gratifications for which many would willingly exchange what to others might appear far higher enjoyments. That a high price is paid for diamonds is of itself sufficient proof, that in some way or other they are capable of affording gratification to those who purchase them: for there is no standard for enjoyment but the opinions of men; and these opinions cannot be more clearly expressed than by the sacrifice of other enjoyments, with regard to the value of which all men are agreed.

Value in use, then, would be the only kind of value connected with the science of Political Economy, were it not necessary to establish various comparisons of wealth, in order to deduce the principles of that science from an extended survey of the world. The capacities of various commodities for the production of enjoyment must be estimated, and the situation of a country at different periods, or of many countries, both at the same and at remote times, must be compared. But it is obviously impossible for the mind to comprehend in one view any considerable portion of the component parts of wealth; and still more impossible so to compare and estimate amounts and uses of objects extremely various and discordant, as to arrive at any general conclusions. To what purpose should we ascertain that one nation possessed so many cattle, another a certain quantity of grain, a third woollens, and a fourth wine, unless we had some means of reducing to one denomination the power of those several articles over the being or well being of man? Or what information should we derive from the nominal amount of the revenue of a state, unless we could form some idea of the quantity of commodities, or rather of the quantity of the means of enjoyment, which that revenue could command?

The necessity of instituting such comparisons makes us have recourse to what has been called *value in exchange.*

Though a variety of dissimilar commodities can neither be classed together in a calculation, nor compared with one another, each of them may be compared with some one article, for which all of them are usually exchangeable. The value in exchange of every description of goods will be ascertained by the quantity of the common commodity which each of them can purchase; and thus the whole wealth of an individual or a nation may be reduced to one common denomination. The relative values of all commodities may in this way be ascertained, and the comparison of their amount, in that article which is taken as the measure of value, will exhibit the various degrees of wealth possessed by several nations at the same period, or by the same country at different times.

In such estimates, those sources of being or enjoyment which are common to all countries, and therefore without exchangeable value, will be altogether disregarded; or if in rare instances, water, which usually belongs to this class, should from its scarcity have acquired exchangeable value, we have only to omit that value in the catalogue of the wealth of such countries, when we institute a comparison between them and more favoured regions. Thus, were we to institute a comparison between the value of a West Indian island in which it had been necessary to construct expensive reservoirs for water, and that of another island enjoying abundance of this necessary of life, we should exclude the value of the reservoirs, and by that means put the islands on an equal footing. This is indeed exactly what would be done by a person who was deliberating whether he should buy an estate in the one island or in the other.

But even of commodities furnished by human industry, it has been said, that the value in exchange is frequently very different from that in use. The degree of scarcity has been represented as so powerful in regulating the former, that by increasing the quantity of the most useful article, you may diminish, in place of increasing, its aggregate value in exchange. By improvements in machinery, the quantity of clothing possessed by a nation may be doubled, although the whole would not exchange for more corn, or wine, or money, than the half of it did before. The value in use has greatly increased, without any corresponding increase in the value in exchange; for were the clothing to be estimated in any other commodity, it would appear to have been stationary, or to have declined in aggregate value, while every individual had become more comfortably or more splendidly dressed. It has therefore been argued that value in exchange, or individual riches, should be carefully distinguished in our reasonings from value in use, or national wealth *.

It is indeed true, that, by changes in manufacturing processes, as well as by changes in

---

* Lauderdale's Inquiry into the Nature and Origin of Public Wealth. Chap. II.

habits, tastes, or fashions, the relative value of different commodities may be greatly altered, and that those persons who happen to be possessed of articles which are produced in larger quantity than formerly, or which, from other circumstances, become less in demand, may find themselves poorer, while the chief uses of the article remain unimpaired. But in such cases, there are others of its uses which cease to exist. Its possession is no longer a mark of distinction, nor can the additional quantity that has been produced, yield to those by whom it must be consumed, gratification equivalent to its former price. Were the price of broad cloth to be reduced one half, and every man to renew his coat twice as often as at present, we might all be better dressed, but not more comfortably; and as all our acquaintances would also wear better coats, even our vanity could derive no additional gratification from the change. The exchangeable value of two coats might now be equal only to what used to be the price of one; but neither would their value in use have experienced any perceptible increase. All of the broad cloth that, in the estimation of purchasers, was worth the former price, had been formerly brought to market, and if more is now to be disposed of, it must be to those who did not reckon its utility equivalent to its former cost. New purchasers indeed will appear in proportion to the reduction of price ; because at every step of the decline it is brought down to the estimate, which an additional number of persons had formed of its power of producing gratification, or in other words, to their estimate of its value in use.

It is a mistake then to consider the value in use of any given quantity of a commodity as unimpaired, when it is brought to market in greater plenty, or when it becomes less in demand ; but it is a still greater mistake to suppose that, while the value in exchange of one commodity is reduced by excess, that of some other commodities will not thereby be enhanced. Those who formerly bought the article that is produced in excess, now getting what they want of it at a lower price, will have part of their revenue to expend in some other way; and the new demand thence arising for some other articles will raise their exchangeable value, in proportion as that of the other is depressed. Were the price of stockings to fall one-half, each person would have half of what he formerly paid for his stockings to expend in shoes, hats, or perhaps in tea or beer, and his increased demand for some of these conveniences or luxuries would advance their value. If, however, the excess of an article at market does not arise from any casual over supply, or from any decrease of the usual demand, but from greater cheapness in its manufacture, no advance in the value of other commodities may take place; because, in such circumstances, their quantity will be augmented in proportion to the new demand for them that has arisen. The manufacturers of the commodity now furnished by an easier and cheaper process will not continue to force it on the market; its production will soon be restricted to what can be sold to advantage; and part of the capital and labour formerly employed in its production will henceforward be directed to the supply of other articles. For these articles a new demand is, at the same time, created by the revenue, now set free, which used to be expended on that commodity, the price of which has been so much reduced. If stockings be made at half price, nearly the half of the labour and capital of the stocking-maker will be turned towards the supply of that new demand for some other kinds of goods, which must arise from the expenditure upon them of half of the revenue that used to go to the purchase of stockings. It will not therefore follow, that, because the exchangeable value of one commodity has declined, that of all the commodities produced by the capital formerly employed in its manufacture, may not have been greatly increased.

When we consider, that by the cheapness of a

particular commodity some of its uses are generally diminished; that by the fall of its price the demand for some other articles, and consequently their prices, are frequently advanced; and that part of the capital and labour, formerly directed to the production of that commodity, is usually withdrawn after an improvement has taken place in its manufacture, and employed in some other kind of production; when we take all those circumstances in connection, we must acknowledge that value in use, whether viewed in reference to any single commodity, or to the aggregate possessions of a nation, must be very accurately measured by value in exchange*.

But it will avail little to have established

---

* I am not aware of any real difference on this subject between M. Say's opinion and mine; though our modes of expression may be a little different. He considers value in exchange as the only kind of value to which the science of Political Economy has reference. To this I agree; but only because it is the *exponent* of value in use or of wealth.

value in exchange as the practical measure both of private and public wealth, unless we can discover some standard by which, at all times and in all places, that value may, with some degree of accuracy, be ascertained. To what purpose should we refer value in use to value in exchange as its measure, unless we have some means of estimating the latter? And among the daily variations in the market-price of every article of merchandise, how are we to estimate the actual exchangeable value of the whole? A standard, to be useful, must be in itself invariable; but of such a standard we have no experience. There is no commodity that ministers to the wants of man which does not fluctuate in its own value, according to the relation which its quantity in the market may bear to the existing demand. There cannot, therefore, be any absolute standard of value; though by selecting a commodity least subject to such variations, and at all times and places in considerable demand, we may perhaps approximate to such a standard sufficiently for the purposes we have in view. That we may do so, however, the commodity must be selected in reference to our immediate object, and varied according to the nature of the inquiry in which we happen to be engaged.

Should we be desirous of comparing two commodities in the same country, and at the same time, the precious metals, in consequence of their being used as the general medium of barter, afford an unexceptionable standard; the money price of an article at a given time and place being, in reference to all commodities at the same time and place, its precise value in exchange. If the comparison be instituted between the same or different commodities at one period of time, but in various countries, this standard requires correction; for the precious metals, from many circumstances, may happen to be in excess in one part of the world, while they are relatively deficient in another. In one place their value will accordingly be lowered, in another it will be raised, in comparison with goods of every description; and the variation in money price, in place of marking a difference in the exchangeable value of commodities, will mark an enhancement or depreciation in the metals themselves. But where there is mutual communication among nations, whether direct or indirect, inequalities in the value of gold and silver in different parts of the world are speedily removed by the operations of commerce; and even while they do exist, they may be accurately measured by attending to the fluctuations of what are called the commercial exchanges.

The difficulty, therefore, is to find a standard applicable to remote periods, experience having proved that the precious metals, from the varying state of the mines, and of the demand created by the extent of commercial transactions, are very ill adapted for this purpose.

Dr Smith was of opinion, that labour is

more uniform in its own value than any commodity, and therefore the best common measure of exchangeable value; but on account of
the impossibility of ascertaining the rate of
wages, at distant times and places, he proposed to substitute corn, by the price of
which he imagined that the rate of wages
was in a great degree influenced. He was
aware that from year to year, this standard was perhaps the most imperfect that could
be chosen; but he thought that, by taking the average of several years, the price of
corn very much coincided with, or rather regulated, that of labour *.

There may perhaps be reason to doubt the
justice of Dr Smith's opinion both of the
invariable value of labour, and of its coincidence, on an average of years, with the
value of corn. That the value of labour varies

Wealth of Nations, Book I. chap. 5.

very greatly seems to be proved, by the great alterations that occur in money-wages, while the value of the precious metals, as ascertained by comparing them with other commodities, has undergone no change. War, by creating a demand for men, raises wages in the nations engaged in hostilities, without affecting them in other countries which remain at peace. The prosperity of a particular manufacture raises wages in one part of the country, while the decay of another branch of trade sinks them in a neighbouring district. Nor are such variations in wages always either temporary or local. In one nation, misgovernment may cause a long and uninterrupted decline of wealth, during the whole of which wages will be extremely depressed; or continued prosperity, during which the demand for labour always precedes the supply, from whatever source that prosperity may be derived, will support wages at a height quite disproportioned to that which they have reached in neighbouring countries. Even then, if we could ascertain the rate of wages in remote times, we should have a measure of value liable, from many circumstances, to great variations.

If corn be adopted as the standard, it cannot be from its coinciding on an average of years with what is so variable in itself as wages; nor, as I shall endeavour to show in the next chapter, does any such coincidence exist. But corn, though fluctuating from year to year more than any other commodity whatever, is perhaps the most steady, if an average be taken of several consecutive years. Were the corn trade entirely free over all the globe, the average value of grain, till the whole earth were fully cultivated, would be nearly the same even at very remote periods, unless it could be supposed that the whole quantity raised in the world did not follow the increase and decrease of the human race*. And even where restrictions on

---

* I must refer to the fourth chapter of this Treatise for illustration of the opinion, that variations in wages and profits,

the freedom of trade prevail, the corn grown or imported will be so proportioned in each country to the number of the inhabitants, that if we take an average sufficiently extensive to include years both of uncommon plenty and uncommon scarcity, it is likely that we shall have as accurate a standard for measuring value in remote periods, as it would be reasonable to expect.

Mr Malthus * has proposed a mean between corn and labour as a still better measure of exchangeable value; and, as I trust I shall be able to show in the next chapter, that though a rise of wages always tends to raise the price of corn, any scarcity of the latter, in place

---

and consequently in the expences of culture, affect rents only, without raising or lowering the value or price of corn, except in so far as they may occasion the substitution of one kind of agricultural produce for another.

* Principles of Political Economy, chap. II. sect. 7.

of raising, always depresses wages, I am inclined to agree to Mr Malthus' opinion. If years of uncommon sterility should raise the price of corn so high as to give a false measure of exchangeable value, wages of labour will at the same time be so far depressed, as to compensate the error, and bring the combined standard considerably nearer to the truth *.

A very different standard of value has been adopted by Mr Ricardo, and made the foundation of an ingenious, but, as it appears to me, an unsound theory †.

The quantity of labour imbodied in a commodity he considers as in all cases its value in exchange; because this quantity of labour must

---

* If the opinion of Dr Smith, adopted by Mr Malthus, that the price of corn regulates wages, were correct, nothing could be gained by joining two standards, which in all situations must be nearly identical.

† Ricardo's Principles of Political Economy, chap. I.

always exchange for an equal quantity of similar labour imbodied in any other article. Allowance indeed must be made for difference both of skill and intensity in the labour employed upon the two articles that are compared; but the relative estimation in which different kinds of labour are held, is nearly the same at all times, and has been adjusted, sufficiently for practical purposes, by the competitions of the market. The profit on the capital employed must likewise be taken into account; but this capital is considered by Mr Ricardo as also entirely resolvable into labour. It is either fixed capital, consisting of implements or machines produced by labour, of which a part, proportioned to the durability of the machine, must be added to the labour directly employed in the production of the commodity; or it is circulating capital, distributed as wages to those who have raised the raw produce, removed it to the place where the manufacture is established, and, after altering its form and properties, again transported it to the place where it is to be consum-

ed.   When all the labour thus directly or indirectly imbodied in a commodity, is fairly
taken into account, we have the whole of its
actual cost, and also its exchangeable value, considered in reference to the labour directly and
indirectly imbodied in any other commodity.

To none of these positions of Mr Ricardo can
I yield my assent.

The capital employed in bringing an article
to market cannot be resolved into wages of labour; its investment being, partly at least, of a
different nature, and the profit which it yields
being regulated by principles quite unconnected
with those which regulate even the wages
which it is the instrument of furnishing to the
workman.   Capital is frequently invested in a
commodity for a very long time, during which it
must yield to its proprietor the ordinary rate of
profit, although it does not, during that period,
give employment to a single person.   The ex-

pence of culture, were we to allow it to be entirely resolvable into wages, is vested in the cotton when it is brought from the field, and may continue so vested for years, yielding its usual annual profit in the ultimate price of the goods, though it never afterwards puts any labour in motion. To this, new capital is added by the transport of the cotton, by its manufacture, and perhaps by its re-exportation to the very place where it was raised. Even if every such addition were made entirely by a farther investment of labour, still the ordinary profit on the capital thus successively imbodied in the article, till the time of its final sale to the consumer, is measured not by labour, but by the length of time that this capital remains vested in the commodity. In this respect, the difference of cost may be very great; for in one article there may be profit on capital for a few days or months, in another for several years. If there be thus an ingredient in cost which cannot be reduced to labour, and which varies very much in different commodities, it would lead to constant error, if we were to take one of the elements of cost as the measure of the whole.

But even if the cost were ascertained, it would not enable us to judge of the exchangeable value. It might indeed give what Dr Smith has called the *natural* price, and Mr Malthus the *necessary* price, of a commodity; that price which repays the rent, profits, and wages necessary to its production, and towards which the market price may be considered as always gravitating. But this is usually very different from exchangeable value. The latter depends entirely on the proportion in the market which the demand for an article may bear to the supply; a proportion ever varying, on the one hand, according to taste, fashion, general or local prosperity, and a thousand other circumstances; and on the other hand, according to the plenty or scarcity of capital or labour, and the fertility of the seasons. Productions are, no doubt, adapted as much as possible to the demand of the consumers; but neither the habits and skill of work-

men, nor the knowledge of merchants and manufacturers, nor least of all, the fixed capital of the
country, can be turned, without great temporary
inconvenience and loss, from the production of
one article to that of another. Every person
continues his usual trade for a considerable
time, even with diminished wages and profits,
especially if the acquired skill of the workmen
cannot be transferred to some other branch of
industry more in demand, or if expensive machinery has been erected, which, by the aban-
donment of a manufacture, would become entirely useless. Equalization of wages and profits is ever in view, but ever unattainable; so
that in the same country, and at the same time,
there could not perhaps be found two articles,
of which the respective costs would be the measure of their respective values.

The difference will be still greater, if we are
comparing different nations or remote periods.
Independently of the innumerable circumstances
affecting the rate of profits and wages in distant

periods and countries, it will usually be found that a rude workman, with ill contrived tools, will take much longer time to execute a piece of very slovenly work, than a good tradesman, with well adapted implements, to finish a very elegant manufacture. The one has not the means of acquiring the taste, the skill, the expertness, or the tools of the other, by any labour, or by any thing that can be measured by labour; depending, as they do, on the habits and general intelligence of a more advanced state of society. But if a coarse article have cost more labour than one that is highly finished, are we, on that account, to say that it is of greater value? or that it should form a larger *item* in our estimate of national wealth?

If, then, the labour actually vested in a commodity can at all be used as a measure of value, it must be in estimating various articles at the same time, and in the same place; a purpose for which we have already a most unexceptionable standard in the precious metals. Besides being extremely vague and inaccurate, the standard proposed by Mr Ricardo is quite unmanageable, when we attempt to apply it to the comparison of the wealth or revenue of separate periods, or of different states.

The cost of a commodity in labour is said to be the work bestowed, not only on its immediate production, but also on the previous education of the workman, and the formation of his tools and machinery*. This last again is resolvable into the direct labour bestowed on the tools, and the indirect on the implements for their construction, and on the education of the tool-maker. This second set of tools, and a third and a fourth, are all capable of the same analysis with the first ; and thus we become engaged in an infinite series. The use of a standard is to simplify comparison, by bringing un-

---

* Ricardo's Principles of Political Economy. Chap. I. sect. 2.

der one denomination an immense number of articles, all of which are portions of national wealth ; but in adopting, as this common designation, the direct and indirect labour employed in their production, we engage, with regard to each individual commodity, in a process more interminable and unsatisfactory, than if we were even to draw out at length the appalling catalogue of all the particulars of the national wealth.

If, on the other hand, we take corn according to its market price as the standard of value, the process, though abundantly perplexing, is comparatively simple. The difficulty indeed remains of getting any thing like a fair account of the existing commodities which constitute the national wealth. Such is the inaccuracy of statistical tables, and of all calculations founded on them, that they must be received with the greatest distrust. But whenever there is reason to confide in them, it is easy to estimate the value of each article in the precious metals, and to correct this defective standard by the money-price of corn, or of labour, or of both. In like manner, when we know the amount of the public revenue in gold, we can have little difficulty in approximating to its power of purchasing corn and labour at any particular time. But were we to attempt, in conformity to Mr Ricardo's theory, to estimate the labour directly and indirectly vested in the innumerable articles on which this revenue is expended, we should involve ourselves in a labyrinth in which we might wander for ever, without acquiring any definite or intelligible notions.

CHAPTER II.

OF WAGES.

THAT the general rate of wages is regulated from day to day by the competition of labourers on the one hand, and of those desirous to employ labourers on the other, is a proposition so plain as to require no proof to any one acquainted with the simplest principles of Political Economy.

It is a competition of a very similar kind that tends to equalize wages among the various employments of the people. Every workman endeavours to get the highest wages that he can;

cvcry cmployer of workmen to get his work done as cheaply as possible. When any branch of business is deficient in hands, the competition of masters raises the wages in that particular branch. In consequence of this, workmen are allured to it from other employments in which the habits and acquirements are somewhat similar, and young men entering into life are led to prefer it to other trades. On the other hand, when an employment is overstocked, the competition for work lowers the wages, and this induces some of the workmen to betake themselves to other kinds of labour in which they can earn better wages, while it prevents young men from engaging in what is known to be an ill paid occupation.

It is thus that whatever casually raises or lowers the wages of one description of labour—whatever affects, in any way, the advantages which it usually possesses in comparison of other kinds of labour, is merely temporary; the ordinary proportions between the several branches of industry in the same country being gradually restored. The rapidity with which this is effected will no doubt depend on the nature of the employment of which the usual advantages have been deranged. From the case with which weaving is learned, this business cannot be understocked without very speedily drawing people even from common country work; but it may continue overstocked for a considerable time, because the habits of a weaver unfit him for any kind of labour that requires exposure to the weather. The business of an engraver may for a long time continue very lucrative, or otherwise; for it requires many years to perfect a workman in this art; and he who has once learned it, even if its usual advantages should be much reduced, will scarcely find it for his interest to betake himself to another occupation: the balance, therefore, can in this case be restored only by the greater or smaller number of young men that may enter into the profession. But whether this equalization among the several employments of labour be more speedily or more slowly effected, there is always a tendency towards it, and it will usually be completed in the course of a few years.

If, therefore, a tax or public burden of any kind be laid on a particular description of labourers, that tax will affect the circumstances of those labourers only for a short time, after which it will occasion a proportional rise in their wages.

But no similar rise of wages will take place if all descriptions of labour be affected in a proportional degree. In this case, the burden, of whatever nature it may be, will rest, where it is originally laid, on the labouring class of the community. The same means of escape do not exist. Let a man change his trade as often as he pleases, the same load will remain upon his shoulders, even if it be such as nearly to crush him to the ground.

All authors are agreed that, in their operation on wages, there is no difference between a tax on labourers, a tax on the necessaries of life, or an enhancement of the value of corn, from whatever circumstances the latter may have arisen. And accordingly almost every writer has considered a rise of wages as a necessary, though not always an immediate, consequence of any one of these occurrences *. It may appear presumptuous in me to dispute what seems thus to be sanctioned by general consent; but my reflections have led me to a very opposite conclusion.

If the rate of wages be entirely regulated by the competition between masters and servants, or more strictly between those desirous of selling and those desirous of purchasing labour, as seems to be universally admitted, it is

---

* It will be sufficient to refer to Dr Smith, Mr Say, Mr Malthus, and Mr Ricardo.

only by influencing this competition, that a tax, or a rise in the price of necessaries, can operate upon wages. That such circumstances can neither increase the capital from which wages are advanced to the workman, nor the demand for the produce of his labour, seems too obvious to require illustration. That they will not diminish the quantity of labour in any one branch, when the burden, affecting them all, cannot be thrown off by change of employment, seems equally obvious; and if this be allowed, the competition must remain undisturbed, and the general rate of wages unvaried. The workman will receive the ordinary remuneration of his labour; but part of it will be taken from him by the tax, or the whole will procure him fewer of the necessaries of life, should their price have been raised; and, exactly in the same degree, his comforts will be abridged.

Dr Smith * has established, beyond the pos-

----

* Wealth of Nations, Book I. chap. 8.

sibility of dispute, that the recompence of labour is mainly dependent on the advancing, stationary, or declining state of a country. If wealth be annually accumulated, the demand for labour will outstrip the supply, and wages will be high : in opposite circumstances, the demand for labour will diminish, and wages must fall. But he seems to have pushed his reasoning too far, when he considered the reward of industry as regulated almost exclusively by the advancing or retrograde state of the country; and therefore laid it down as a general principle, that whatever tended to diminish the efficiency of his wages in commanding the necessaries of life, must be compensated to the workman, by a rise in their nominal amount.

Let us suppose a capitation tax of a shilling a week to be levied from every inhabitant, and see in what manner a labourer could contrive to throw this tax on his employer. Before the imposition of the tax, there were certain funds for the payment of labour, and a certain number of men desirous of working for hire, and wages would be liberal or scanty, according to the proportion that those funds bore to the population. As the tax in no respect disturbs that proportion, it can have no effect whatever upon wages; for if more of the fund be given to one workman, it is plain that less would remain for the others, who must either, in such a case, submit to a reduction of their wages, or remain unemployed. There is therefore no way in which the labourer could continue, by devolving the burden on his employers, to live as comfortably as before the imposition of the tax.

The operation of a rise in the price of corn, resembles in every respect a capitation tax. There were certain funds destined to the purchase of the food of all the labourers in the country. If, in consequence of a rise in the price of corn, these funds will purchase less of it than formerly, while the number of people desirous of exchanging their labour for corn is undiminished, each workman must content himself with a smaller quantity of that article, or some of them must be unable to procure food in exchange for their work. This latter alternative cannot take place, as those who were thrown out of employment would offer to work on lower terms; and the others, who insisted on getting as much corn as before, would soon be obliged to conform to the rate fixed by the general competition.

That the exchange between corn and labour is effected by means of money, does not alter the case; for while the quantity of labour bears its former proportion to the currency, and therefore bears its former money price, corn, for which it is ultimately to be exchanged, has advanced, whether it be estimated in that currency or in labour.

It is perfectly true, as stated by Dr Smith, that wages consist not in the money, but in what the money will purchase; but it seems to have escaped him that the very same observation is applicable to the capital from which wages are advanced, and to the revenues from the expenditure of which they are ultimately paid. When the necessaries of life become scarcer and dearer, less of them can be procured for the same amount of capital or revenue, and therefore that capital and revenue can furnish less of them to the labourers whom they employ.

Had Dr Smith's reasoning been just, it might have been inferred that a rise in the price of such luxuries as are consumed by the common people would be attended with exactly the same consequences as a rise in the necessaries of life; for the comforts of a workman, equally with his subsistence, are assigned to him by the demand existing for his labour, according to the advancing, stationary, or declining condition of the country. That this is not the case was too obvious to be denied, no one having ever imagined that a tax on spirits, or tea, or sugar, or the enhancement of those articles of luxury during a war, had the slightest effect on the rate of wages. Dr Smith therefore was driven to a distinction much more specious than solid, between the necessaries and luxuries consumed by the people*. Whatever affects the former, he considers as necessarily affecting wages, while a tax on luxuries has no such result; and the reason he assigns is that luxuries are not essential to the rearing of a family. This distinction, however, he has not always kept in view; for if it were well founded, taxes on labour would not fall entirely on the employers of labour, as he has taught; but partly on them, and partly on the workmen, according to the proportion of wages usually spent on necessaries and on luxuries respectively.

To support this distinction, it must be assumed, that the economy practised in consequence of the dearness of any commodity is usually

---

* Wealth of Nations, Book V. chap. ii. Part ii. art. 4,

confined to that particular commodity; that a rise in the price of wine occasions a diminished consumption only of wine; that a rise in the price of bread produces economy only of food. But this is so far from being the case, that a tax on tobacco will induce one man to restrict the use of spirits, another of butcher meat, and a third of clothes, and ma.. to spread the privations to which they must submit, in different proportions, over a great variety of articles. No workman, or indeed any other person, makes a formal distribution of his income between necessaries and luxuries; far less would he abide by this distribution, if a change of circumstances should make him desirous of altering the proportion assigned to each. Whichever of those parts of his expenditure might be directly affected, his conduct would be precisely the same. A fall in his wages, a tax on his labour, a high price of corn, will induce the well-doing to give up such comforts as are most easily dispensed with, rather than expose their children to cold and hunger ; while a diminution of income, or a rise in the price of gin, will tempt the profligate to starve their families, rather than relinquish their own vicious indulgences. With the one class, every diminution of income will have the effect ascribed to a tax on luxuries; with the other, that which is said to attend a tax on the necessaries of life.

If this be a true representation, Dr Smith's distinction must be abandoned, and with it the position that taxes on labour, and high price of the necessaries of life, by raising wages, fall on the employers of the labourers; unless indeed we are prepared to say, that whatever affects the labourer's condition, his command either of necessaries or luxuries, must in the same degree heighten his money-wages.

So far is this from being the case, that the first consequence of a scarcity of corn is to lower, not to raise, the money price of labour. In place of relinquishing their usual comforts, or abridging the food of their children, many of

the industrious increase the intensity or duration of their labour, and some of those, who
were formerly accustomed to pass part of the
day or of the week in dissipation, apply more
steadily to work. The quantity of labour at
market is thus, for a time at least, increased as
its remuneration is diminished; and the capital
and expenditure of the country having undergone no similar change, there is a want of effective demand for the extra labour pressed upon
the market, and wages fall in money price, at
the very time, when, if Dr Smith's opinion
were correct, they must inevitably have advanced. That this takes place is known to every
one at all engaged in manufactures, and has indeed been stated by Dr Smith himself *, though
he perhaps was not aware of the extent to
which it operates. It is more remarkable that
the same thing occurs, even when wages have

* Wealth of Nations, Book I. chap. 8.

been lowered in consequence of a decrease in consumption and demand. Those workmen who, from favour, or good behaviour, or skill, can still procure employment, increase their hours of labour, that they may enjoy their usual income, and thus add to that glut in the market from which they and their fellow-workmen are already suffering *.

It is true, that this effect of whatever deteriorates the condition of the labouring classes is only temporary. By degrees workmen revert to their usual hours of labour, and their usual degree of application; but as they are not likely to slacken their diligence, when it is more than usually necessary to their comfort, the quantity

---

* Some masters are at pains to prevent this; but others, as might be expected, avail themselves of the opportunity of getting more of their work performed at low rates, and by the best hands.

of labour at market is not at any time diminished; and, therefore, in place of raising their
wages, they are forced to dispense with some of
their little comforts or indulgences.

To this, no doubt, there is a limit. If the
common people are rendered unable to rear their
families, population must decline; and when,
in consequence of famine and disease, the quantity of labour at market has been diminished,
its remuneration will improve. But happily
there are few countries in which the people are
in so wretched a state, that such a calamity,
except in very extraordinary circumstances, can
be apprehended. That in Britain there is nothing, in ordinary times, approaching to such a
state, Dr Smith has proved by reasons equally
applicable to the present as to former times *,
if indeed any proof were requisite of what

* Wealth of Nations, Book I. chap. 8.

every person must know to be true. Even in Ireland, where a long course of foreign oppression and domestic misrule has reduced the peasantry to a state of misery rarely to be met with in Europe, the people, so far from having been incapacitated by that misery from rearing families, have increased their numbers in a most remarkable degree. With regard to countries, then, in which the state of the people is incomparably superior to that of the Irish peasantry, we may be assured that that limit is still distant, beyond which every tax on labour, and every rise on the price of food, must be followed by the destruction of life, and, through it, by a proportional improvement in the condition of the survivors.

Mr Malthus, in his desire to enforce truths which he considered as most important to the welfare of mankind, has often expressed an opinion that, both in the ancient and modern world, population has very generally pressed hard on the means of subsistence *. The expression, as it is frequently qualified by him, ought rather to have been, that population has pressed hard on the comforts of the people; a truth which every benevolent man will regret, though he may doubt whether a reduction of the numbers of the people might not increase, rather than alleviate, the evil. But if we are required to assent to the proposition, as it is usually stated by Mr Malthus, we must first understand correctly what it is meant to convey.

If it be meant that there is little or no surplus of food, but that all that is produced is in ordinary years consumed; this is true, and always will be so, not only of food, but of every other commodity. There is no inducement to produce corn, more than hats or shoes, beyond the ordinary consumption; and were you to double the rate of wages, or reduce the number of people to one half, population would, in

* Essay on Population, throughout.

this sense, still press on the means of subsistence*.

Again, if it be meant, that a great proportion of labourers spend the whole of their earnings, without reserving any thing for years of sickness, of scarcity, or of bad trade; and that, in consequence of this, they are occasionally exposed to severe hardships; this also is true, and much to be regretted. But it amounts to nothing more than the very common observation, that many people live fully up to their incomes,

---

* I cannot, therefore, agree with Mr Malthus, that an increase of food must usually precede an increase of population; for such an increase of food beyond the demand must be purely accidental. It seems probable, that for the most part, high wages occasion some little increase of population, and at the same time less economy in the use of food: hence a high price of corn, and soon after, an increased supply. The question, however, is of little importance, as whichever may have the priority, the one cannot continue long without the other. Population cannot continue to increase in any country, without an increase of food grown or imported; nor will an extra quantity of corn be raised, unless there be more people to consume it.

an observation applicable to the rich as well as to the poor; though the former are not always so severely punished for their imprudence.

But if it be meant, either that the present number of people could not be maintained on lower wages, or that a much greater number could not be supported on the present wages, no proposition can be more directly at variance with matter of fact*. The people in almost every nation of Europe, enjoy some little comforts in their dress, food, or habitations, which, by injudicious taxes, or bad seasons, they might be forced to relinquish, not indeed without suffering great misery, but without either themselves or their children being deprived of life.

There is, however, a more gradual manner in which it has been thought, that, long before it be-

---

* Of course I must not be understood as referring to the late very uncommon depression of wages, for which I shall afterwards endeavour to account.

comes physically impossible for the people to maintain their numbers, the difficulty of subsistence will have the effect of discouraging population. That degree of comfort to which a man has been accustomed he does not easily relinquish. Whatever his situation in life may be, it is hard to give up habitual indulgences, and still harder to exhibit to neighbours and friends the appearances of indigence and decay. But as we descend in the scale of wealth and rank, the intensity of this hardship is always increased. He may easily part with a few luxuries, who has almost every real comfort remaining, and who, by more rigid economy in his family, or by a life of greater privacy, may conceal the decay of his fortune from the public eye. But every little indulgence wrung from a poor man materially injures his real welfare; and the disappearance of his furniture, the decay of his clothes, perhaps the emaciation of his countenance, proclaim the calamity that has befallen him.

While thus suffering under privations, and witnessing the still greater sufferings of his married friends, it may be expected that a young man will be unwilling to charge himself with the expence of a family, and that fewer marriages being contracted, fewer children will be born, and population will gradually decline.

That such, for a time, will be the consequence of any very sudden deterioration of the circumstances of the labouring class, there can be no doubt; but both the extent and duration of its effect on population, and through it on wages, seem of late to have been very much exaggerated. He who is desirous of marrying is not in the state of mind most favourable to rigid calculation. Sacrifices of personal indulgence he must have laid his account with; and whether these sacrifices be a little more or a little less than usual, he will not very scrupulously examine. If he has been able to lay up a little money for the purchase of furniture, he may devote a portion of it to eke out for a time his reduced income; and he will be very much un-like the rest of mankind, if he be not sanguine enough to believe that the bad trade or bad harvest, to which he ascribes his present difficulties, will soon be succeeded by prosperity and plenty.

But if, for a short time, marriages should be discouraged, it will be many years before this circumstance can at all be perceptible upon wages. The children that might have been born from marriages so postponed or prevented will bear a very slender proportion to those issuing from marriages already contracted; and even this slight reduction of population cannot influence wages for fifteen or sixteen years, previously to which the labour of those children would be of little value. Long before such a period has elapsed, many variations are likely to have occurred in the condition of labourers. A plentiful season will have lowered the price of food, or some casual demand will have occasioned a temporary rise of wages. Flattering themselves that the improvement in their circumstances may be permanent, and feeling that it is now in their power to gratify their wishes, many who had been forced to delay their marriages will fulfil their engagements; and the check to population, in so far as they are concerned, will be entirely at an end.

Even if no favourable seasons have occurred, the check is in its own nature merely temporary. The habits of men change with their circumstances, and those who for years have been accustomed to inferior comforts, gradually cease to expect their former indulgences. A young man, in contracting marriage, will propose to maintain his family in the same style that his relations and acquaintances now live; not in that which he is informed, or perhaps may remember, they could afford in past times; and whenever this is in his power, he is no longer restrained by the general reduction that has taken place in the circumstances of the people.

The only consequence of the taxation of the lower orders, or the enhancement of the price of necessaries, that in its own nature is permanent, is the retrenchment of some of the comforts of the people; a retrenchment which they cannot avoid by directly raising their wages, and from which it would be mockery to desire them to expect relief by the discouragement of marriage, and the consequent, though confessedly very distant and contingent, decay of population. How far this deterioration in their circumstances may be carried by injudicious or oppressive measures, it is impossible to say. It is bounded, indeed, at that point, at which it becomes impossible for a labourer, by his utmost industry, to rear his family. But there can be no greater mistake in political reasoning, though it is by no means an uncommon one, than to assume, that what forms an ultimate limit necessarily acts as a regular or progressive check. We need only refer to Ireland, to be convinced that a state of poverty which, if pushed a little farther, would necessarily and directly diminish the population, has hitherto had little effect in preventing its increase, even though the people have been reduced to the utmost misery and abasement.

Considering the powerful passions that lead to marriage, we shall not be surprised that prosperity has a much more decided effect in promoting population, than adversity in discouraging it. When a man is easy in his circumstances, he looks round for additional enjoyments, among which marriage will always hold a distinguished place. When he is straitened, he abstains from some enjoyment; but it will depend on the strength of his passion whether he will refrain from marriage, or deny himself some other gratifications. We must consider, too, that a marriage contracted in favourable times, is a source of population that continues to flow, even should the circumstances of the country be changed. But a marriage postponed, if it afterwards take place, may be as prolific as if it had been contracted at a somewhat earlier period. It has, therefore, been truly stated by Dr Smith, that, to secure a liberal reward to labour, national wealth must be progressive; and that whenever, by its becoming stationary, the demand for labour no longer precedes the supply, the rate of wages is speedily reduced. It is not the amount of national wealth, but its increase from year to year, that diffuses affluence among the people*.

I am far from denying Mr Malthus' positions, that elevation of character in the lower classes very powerfully retards their descent from the degree of comfort which they have been accustomed to enjoy, and that the most efficient circumstances for the production of such a character, are civil and political liberty,

* Wealth of Nations, Book I. chap. 8.

and education*. A free and high spirited people will exert every nerve to escape what they consider as degradation, and by superior ingenuity and energy, they will often succeed. By superior prudence too, they will sometimes alleviate those privations which they cannot altogether avoid; and feeling keenly the loss of former comforts associated in their minds with personal respectability, they will be less apt to aggravate the evil by imprudent marriages. This feeling of degradation, however, which is by far the most powerful check on marriage, like all the other checks, is of a temporary nature. It is not any particular degree of comfort that is requisite to self respect, but that degree of it which is enjoyed by reputable people of the same rank. If all be equally reduced, none can feel degraded, and consequently, whenever an inferior style of living

---

* Principles of Political Economy, chap. 4. sect. 2.

has become common, this check on population also will cease to operate.

It seems then impossible to deny, that by low wages, high prices of necessaries, or grinding taxes, the habits of even the freest nation may be gradually brought down ; and that, by opposite circumstances, those of an ignorant and oppressed people will be gradually raised. Neither, in the one case, will the taxes on labour, or the dearness of food, so far discourage population as to affect very materially the rate of wages; nor, in the other, will the affluence of the lower orders fail to inspire desires for superior dress, food, and accommodations.

It seems a very unreasonable apprehension, that the cheapness of provisions will, in any case, contribute to the degradation of a people. When a labourer's wages are more than is requisite to the subsistence of his family, whether this arise from high wages or cheap food, he will naturally spend the surplus in some additional gratifications, which, if he can afford them for a sufficient length of time, will come to be ranked among the comforts required for his respectability. Unmarried labourers will be induced to marry only when they can procure those customary comforts for their families; and though some may be so imprudent as merely to look to the possibility of bare subsistence, it is likely that they would act in the same manner, whatever might be the cause which enabled them to procure those necessaries. Additional demand for labour and high wages will, in this respect, have precisely the same effect with cheapness of provisions; but it would sound somewhat oddly to warn the people against high wages, as a powerful cause of indigence and misery.

The state of Ireland is always appealed to on this subject; but the cause of the wretchedness of the peasantry of that unhappy country must be sought in an oppressive government, not in the culture of the potatoe. If that government have deprived the people of all security, of all justice, and of all sentiments of self respect, population would naturally be pushed to the limits of subsistence, although no cheaper food were known than the finest wheat. In the north of Ireland, the continued progress of manufactures has kept wages at a higher rate than in the west and south; and, though population has advanced very rapidly, and the potatoe is in general use, the comforts of the people are greatly superior to those in other parts of the island. In like manner, the improvement in the habits of the Scots began in the manufacturing districts, where wages were highest, and gradually spread to other parts of the country, as the demand for labour increased. Notwithstanding the economical habits of the Scots, no person has imagined that the extensive culture of the potatoe has there had any of the disastrous consequences attributed to it in Ireland. On the contrary, exactly like an advance of wages, it has left to the labourer a larger sum to expend on clothes and furniture, or to lay up, as a reserve for his future wants, and the means of raising his sons to professions superior to his own.

If the potatoe yield a wholesome nourishment, its cheapness is, in every view, a high recommendation. In a prosperous country, it either enables a greater number to exist in a manner equally comfortable (for many prefer the potatoe to bread), or it enables the same number of inhabitants to enjoy some additional luxuries, or it puts it in their power to add to their wealth. Even in a declining country, it removes to some distance that lowest state of existence, in which the people, by their utmost exertions, can merely prolong a miserable life. If such a life be, upon the whole, a curse, it no doubt extends it to a greater number; but it occasions no additional suffering to any individual; for a man half starved on wheat is little happier than he who is half starved on potatoes.

It is said, indeed, that a nation accustomed to superior food has a great resource in times of scarcity, by descending to an inferior kind of nourishment. But those who have used this argument seem to have forgot, that unless the potatoe were at all times used by the people, less of it would be raised, and when, from the pressure of want, it came into demand, none of it could be procured.

These reflections, I confess, have left no doubt upon my own mind, that it ought to be received as a fundamental principle in Political Economy, that independently of variations in the value of gold and silver, the price of labour is regulated solely by the demand for it, and in no degree, as taught by Dr Smith, and adopted from him by modern authors, either by the price of the necessaries of life, or by the taxes that may be laid directly or indirectly on necessaries or labour *.

With regard to taxes on labour, Mr Ricardo has advanced an argument which must be ascribed to that inadvertency for which all authors, on abstruse questions, are entitled to indulgence. If such taxes did not raise the rate of wages, the former employers of labour would have their funds unimpaired, while government, in expending the revenue arising from the tax, would create a new demand for labour. In this way, even if wages did not rise on the imposition of the tax, he imagines that they must

---

* The opinions which I have now endeavoured to establish, will be found somewhat differently stated and illustrated in Elements of Political Science, Book II. chap. 4. sect. 5. ; and Book III. Part. ii. chap. 2. sect. 1.

Mr Buchanan, in his Notes on the Wealth of Nations, a work published almost at the same time with mine, has enforced the same doctrines with much ingenuity and success.

speedily advance in consequence of the increased competition of employers*.

To the greater part of the revenue of Britain, required for paying the interest of debt the capital of which has long ago been spent, this argument has no reference; and with regard to the rest of it, Mr Ricardo has for a moment forgot, that wages, at least in an equal degree with the rest of the private or public revenue of the country, by their expenditure, create a demand for labour.

It is of infinite importance that we should form correct opinions regarding the operation of

---

* " If labour were not to rise when wages are taxed, " there would be a great increase in the competition for la- " bour, because the owners of capital, who have nothing to " pay towards such a tax, would have the same funds for em- " ploying labour, whilst the government who received the " tax, would have an additional fund for the same pur- " pose."—Principles of Political Economy and Taxation, chap. 16.

taxes on labour, or on the necessaries of life. Were the doctrine true, that all such taxes occasion a corresponding rise on wages, it might probably be shewn that the wants of the state could be supplied in no way more economical or more just. The various classes of inhabitants, consuming the produce of labour very nearly in proportion to their respective expenditures, would thus be taxed as nearly as can be expected, according to their respective wealth. This has been formally stated by Mr Ricardo *, and no opinion is likely to meet a more cordial reception from a minister of finance; such taxes being of all others the cheapest in collection, and the most certain in their produce. Indeed, it is to the prevalence of such errors, that, in fairness, we must ascribe the selection of taxes lately imposed in Britain†.

At a time when, from other causes, wages

---

* Principles of Political Economy and Taxation, chap. 9.
† Budget 1819.

were so far depressed that the family of every
workman in the country was suffering the severest privations, it is not otherwise conceivable
that any minister should have proposed, or any
House of Commons should have sanctioned,
the imposition of new taxes, every one of
which affected some of the comforts of those
who were already oppressed. Taxes on the
few gratifications enjoyed by the poor, are always unjust; but in such circumstances, had
there not been a vague belief that what was
nominally levied from the poor, would be ultimately paid by the rich, it is surely a very moderate tribute to the humanity of the legislature to say, that such a proposal, if it ever
could have been made, would have been in-
stantly rejected with generous indignation.

CHAPTER III.

OF PROFIT.

WHEN a person has accumulated wealth, he may lay it up as a provision for his own enjoyment at a future time, in which case it can yield him no sort of profit or increase; or he may employ it as capital, in advancing maintenance to workmen, till such time as the produce of their labour can be sold to him by whom it is to be enjoyed, in procuring the raw material on which they are to work, in providing the necessary implements, in sending the finished goods to the best market, and in exchanging the superfluities of one country for those of another.

Independently of the risk attendant on all such transactions, every man would retain his wealth under his own power, and ready to minister to his own gratification, if he did not expect some kind of advantage from employing it as capital. This advantage, in whatever it may consist, is the profit which he derives from his capital; and it is not difficult to see in what manner such profit may accrue to him without occasioning loss to any other person.

If he employ his stock in agriculture, the excess of the produce of the land over what has been consumed by the labourers and cattle, or expended in repairing the agricultural implements (with the exception of the rent, to be considered in the next chapter), is the profit of the farmer. That this profit arises from the employment of his capital, and adds to his wealth without diminishing that of any other person, is abundantly obvious.

If, in place of farming, the possessor of capital should employ it in manufacture, he will be able to finish some commodity at a much less expence, and of much superior quality, than if he who wanted the commodity were obliged first to go in quest of the raw material, and afterwards of a workman. This the manufacturer can do by the division of labour which he introduces into his process, and by the invention and employment of various machines; advantages that arise from the regular employment of his capital, and which no person occasionally making the article for his own use, could possibly enjoy. Besides, the consumer gets the commodity when he wants it, in place of waiting till it be made; he sees that it is exactly suited to his purpose, in place of being liable, in this respect, to disappointment; and he has the advantage of the experience of the master manufacturer, both in providing the raw material, and in getting the work done on the best terms. For all these accommodations, he would be willing to pay, if necessary, even more than it would cost him to have the article made at home. On the other hand, the workman, on account of regular and constant work, is willing to abate part of the wages which he might procure from those who had occasion on their own account for his services ; being sensible that his gains would be reduced in a much greater degree, by frequent loss of time in seeking out new employers. Manufacturing profits, independently of the division of labour and invention of superior machines, may thus be derived from capital, without diminishing the means of enjoyment possessed by any member of the community.

The merchant, by his knowledge of markets, by removing from one place what, in consequence of its plenty, is cheap, and carrying it to another, where, in consequence of its scarcity, it is dear, adds to the value of commodities more than the expence of the carriage; and this addition constitutes his profit. Wine becomes of greater value by being brought to Britain, and cotton goods by being sent to Portugal *. Every purchaser in both countries gets what he considers as an equivalent for the money that he pays, for otherwise he would not purchase at all; but by the rise of value occasioned by the transport of the goods, the merchant receives more for each cargo than it had cost, and thus is enriched, while none of his customers is impoverished.

The purchaser might no doubt have sent to the country where the commodity that he wanted was cheap; and thus he might have supplied

---

* This is true both of value in use, and value in exchange. The wine in England gives more gratification either to taste or vanity than it could have done in Portugal, and solely in consequence of this it sells at a higher price.

himself at a lower rate, without the interven-
tion of the merchant.   But had he done so, he
must, in most cases, have paid for the article before he required it, which he could have done
only by withdrawing some of his own capital
from a profitable employment : he might not
have got the article at the time he wished, or it
might not have been exactly fit for his purpose :
and it is seldom that he would be able to judge
correctly in what market he might procure it
cheapest and best.   The same difficulties would
prevent the seller of the commodity from sending it, at his own risk, to the market where it
happened to be in demand.   Both buyer and
seller, therefore, find it for their interest to resign to the merchant that profit on the commodity which is the exact measure of the addition
made to its value by change of place, content-
ing themselves, the one to receive, and the
other to pay, its market price, where they respectively reside.   By doing so, they lose nothing that they were possessed of; but the mer-

chant receives in the increased value, a compensation for his risk, and a profit on the capital he had employed*.

---

*˙ In speaking of profit, it should always be kept in view, that what is frequently classed under that name, is in part wages of the labour of the person who conducts the business. This has been sufficiently explained by Dr Smith in his Wealth of Nations, Book I. chap. 10. Part. i.

The interest of capital, which may belong either to the merchant or to his creditor, might also be distinguished from those other parts of commercial profit that accrue to the individual or company carrying on the trade [*L'Entre preneur,* in the language of Mr Say]. This last, which every merchant considers as his *net profit,* is in all cases a compensation for risk, which, on an average of years, must exceed that risk ; it is also in farming and manufactures a compensation for the farther risk attending the fixing of capital in implements and machinery, and in the latter for the various arrangements which permit the introduction of a division of labour ; in foreign trade, for the establishment of magazines and connections at home, and of correspondences or branches abroad ; and in the retail trade, for the establishment of credits in the best markets for purchasing, and for the acquisition of safe and regular customers [the good will of the shop]. In balancing the affairs of a commercial company, the salaries of the acting partners, and the interest of the capital employed, to whomever it may belong, are deducted, before that profit be declared, which is divided among the partners according to the shares they

In whatever way, then, capital be vested, its profit is always limited by the addition actually made by its employment to the value of a commodity, over and above the actual cost of altering the form of that commodity, or removing it from one place to another. But though this be the limit of profit, it is very far from being its measure; the competition of capital for the most advantageous investiture always reducing profits greatly under this limit, and producing a tendency to equalization among the various employments of stock.

For a short time, a person who has discovered a superior manufacturing process, or a new market for his goods, may enjoy a very lucrative trade, because he may produce his commodities at little cost, or sell them at an extravagant

---

hold in the concern. As, however, the ordinary rate of interest usually depends on the ordinary rate of profit, and would always do so, were the usury law repealed, it is not perhaps very material to keep them apart in our reasonings.

price. But such gains are of a very temporary nature. His neighbours, vigilant where their interests are so nearly concerned, will soon imitate his fabrics, and ship goods of a similar kind to the same ports. The quantity of the commodity produced and sent to the favourable market will in a short time become equal, or perhaps superior, to the demand, and the high profits will gradually sink to the level, or perhaps below the level, of those derived from ordinary trades.

There is therefore, in the various employments of stock, a constant tendency to equalization in the rate of profit, similar to the tendency to equalization, formerly noticed, in the wages of the several descriptions of labour. As a workman is always unwilling to change his employment, and indeed can seldom do so without considerable disadvantage, so also he who happens to be engaged in a trade that has become unprofitable, may continue it for a considerable time, partly from disinclination to change, partly from the hope of its improvement, chiefly because his habits, knowledge, and establishments, enable him to conduct it with little trouble or superior advantage. But a young man entering into business fixes upon that branch in which there seems the best prospect of success; and thus, independently of the removal of capital already vested, a certain degree of equality among profits is produced, which a thousand circumstances are always disturbing, and the interests of merchants always tending to restore.

There is, however, one description of capital, and that of great amount in an opulent country, the profits of which are, only in particular circumstances, equalized with those of other kinds of stock. I allude to fixed capital, which is vested in implements and machines useful in the production of articles of consumption. Between *fixed* and *circulating* capital, there are two essential differences, which cannot be disregarded without danger of our being betrayed into false conclusions in finance and commercial legislation.

1*st*, Fixed capital does not minister directly to the wants or pleasures of man ; while circulating capital is vested in articles which are in themselves objects of his desire, and which, in yielding him enjoyment, are more or less quickly consumed *.

2*dly*, Fixed capital yields its profit without passing away from its present owner ; while articles in which circulating capital is vested produce no profit, except at the moment when they are sold or exchanged †.

The business of cotton-spinning may suffi-

---

* See Elements of Political Science, Book II. chap. 4. sect. 2. where this distinction is more fully illustrated.

† Wealth of Nations, Book. II. chap. 1.

ciently illustrate the distinctions between fixed and circulating capital. The machinery of a cotton mill is not directly the object of human desire, nor does it directly supply human wants; and, by the work which it performs, it enriches its proprietor without at any time passing out of his possession. But the cotton goods directly supply human wants, in doing which they are consumed; and they produce profit, only at the time of passing by sale from the hands of one person to those of another*.

In consequence of those peculiarities in the nature of fixed capital, its profits have not, in all circumstances, that tendency to equalization,

---

* Mr Ricardo's distinction between fixed and circulating capital is very different. " According as capital is rapidly " perishable, and requires to be frequently reproduced, or is " of slow consumption, it is classed under the heads of circu- " lating or of fixed capital."—Principles of Political Economy and Taxation, chap. 1.—Well might he add, after giving this definition, " A division not essential, and in which the " line of demarcation cannot be accurately drawn."

either among themselves, or as compared with other profits, which has been remarked in those derived from circulating capital. As the articles in which circulating capital is vested must necessarily pass at last into the hands of the consumer, and be paid for, not by other capital, but by funds destined to unproductive expenditure, an opportunity is offered, at every such time, of withdrawing stock from a disadvantageous investment, and directing it to some other employment. If the hat-maker find his trade a bad one, he will replace only a part of those hats which he has disposed of to the retailer, who again will employ a part of the money which he receives for hats from his customers, in laying in some other article more in demand. But there is no similar power of withdrawing fixed capital from its actual investment. A cotton mill, however frequently it may be sold, not being wanted by the purchaser for his own gratification, is never paid for out of the funds destined for his own expenditure. At each sale it absorbs as much capital as it sets free, and after the transference, neither is there less machinery in the country, nor less produce from that machinery.

While the demand is increasing for an article produced by fixed capital, and new machinery of the same description is wanted to meet this demand, the profits of fixed capital will undoubtedly be regulated in a great degree by those of other branches of trade. If its profits be higher, more capital will be fixed in machinery, till the manufactured article fall to such a price as will pay the ordinary profit, and nothing more, on the cost of the machines. Should the business be overdone for a time, and its profits be lower than this, no new machinery of that description will be erected, till the gradually advancing demand for its produce has again raised its returns fully as high as those derived from other employments of stock.

But it is quite otherwise when the demand for the produce of the machinery is declining.

The stock that has been fixed in it can never afterwards be withdrawn; the quantity of goods that it brings forward for sale cannot, without sacrificing the capital, be diminished; and, therefore, even at a time when other branches of trade are in a flourishing condition, there is no limit short of absolute zero, to the possible decrease of profit derived from fixed capital. A change of fashion, the interruption of trade by war, an impolitic regulation at home, or an illiberal prohibition by a foreign state, may for years reduce the profit, or may even annihilate the value, of capital that had been fixed in machinery with the most flattering prospect of success. And this is a risk from which circulating capital, by its own nature, is entirely exempt.

It is a consequence of the same competition which tends to equalize profits arising from circulating capital, that taxes affecting such profits sometimes fall ultimately on the possessors of capital, but more frequently on the consumers of the goods manufactured or imported. The principles, according to which they ultimately affect the one or the other class of inhabitants, are indeed very analogous to those by which the operations of taxes on industry are regulated.

If every description of capital be equally taxed, as was intended to be done by the late property tax, there can be no corresponding rise on profits. The tax makes no alteration, either on the quantity of capital in the country, or on the demand for the goods which it manufactures or imports. Nor is there any means of escaping from the charge, by changing the nature of the investment of stock. Every thing remaining as before, profits can undergo no variation, and the tax will ultimately rest, where it is originally laid, on the capitalist. To this there is no exception, unless the capital itself, by the heaviness of the imposition, be driven out of the country; in which case, from the diminution of its quantity, while the uses of it are very little, if at all, abridged, the general rate of profit will advance.

But when any particular branch of trade is taxed more highly than others, in whatever way the burden may be imposed, the profits of that trade will rise sufficiently to compensate the tax, and place its clear profit on a level with that of other employments of stock. This is the necessary result of the watchful care of merchants in seeking out and preferring the most lucrative employments; and it is not difficult to trace the manner in which self-interest diminishes the supply of the article that has been taxed, while the demand for it continues unabated. In most cases, indeed, the tax itself absorbs part of the capital which had formerly been employed in bringing the commodity to market. If a duty be laid on the manufacture of hats, part of the capital with which skins were purchased, or wages paid, must be diverted from manufacture to the payment of the tax, and fewer hats being afterwards brought to market by the same capital, their price will rise, In like manner, should a duty be laid on tobacco, the merchant can import less of it than formerly by the employment of the same stock, and in proportion to its scarcity, the value of tobacco will advance.

Even before this circumstance has time to operate, an advance of price, in consequence of a new tax, may, and usually does, take place. But this also arises from a diminution of supply, while the demand remains unaltered, Dealers foreseeing that such an advance may in a short time be expected, and desirous of securing it on the stock of goods in their possession, become unwilling to sell on their former terms, and by keeping back their goods from the market, produce an artificial scarcity, the consequences of which are precisely the same with those of a diminished supply.

It frequently indeed happens, that the high price of a commodity discourages its consumption in a degree equal, or more than equal, to that in which its supply is at first diminished. In this case, some of the dealers are likely to abandon the trade; but even if they should all continue in it, they will be less desirous of borrowing money in order to extend their transactions; the slowness of their sales will render their capitals less effective in supplying the market; and when they die or retire from business, their places will be unoccupied, till the diminution of supply has again restored the profit on the commodity to the ordinary rate. That for a time, and only for a time, a new tax is disadvantageous to a merchant or manufacturer, may be conjectured from the violence with which at first he opposes every increase of duty on those articles in which he deals, and the good humour with which he afterwards acquiesces in what he had loudly proclaimed to be the utter ruin of his trade.

A tax on machinery, or on its produce, may, or may not, affect the price of the manufactured article. If there be a demand for more machines of the same kind, prices must rise at least to the ordinary level after paying the tax, before other persons will be induced to change circulating into fixed capital. If, on the other hand, the machinery have outstript, or even equalled, the demand for its produce, the tax will be a deduction from the already depressed profits of the manufacturer, which, until part of the existing machinery be worn out, he has no means of devolving on the purchaser of his goods.

From having adopted the cost in labour as the standard of value, Mr Ricardo has been led to the conclusion, that profits are in the inverse ratio of wages; so that not only do the former decline as the latter advance, but the rise of the one, during the progress of national wealth, is the efficient cause of the diminution of the other.

The value of agricultural produce may be resolved into the wages of labour, the profit on the farming stock, and the landlord's rent. The amount of the latter, according to Mr Ricardo's views, which will be more particularly examined in the next chapter, depends upon the difference in fertility between the lands in culture, and those which merely pay wages and profit without yielding any return to the proprietor; and this portion of the value of the produce is quite unconnected with the rate of wages, and indeed independent of every thing except the relative fertility of the several lands that are cultivated. Deducting rent, therefore, the rest of the produce is divided between wages and profits; and whatever increases the share of the one must evidently to the same degree diminish that of the other. But it is universally agreed, that the rate of profit is equalized in the several employments of stock; and consequently, if farming profit be reduced by a rise in

wages, all other profits must experience a similar decline*.

It is rather a startling circumstance attending this theory, that what it represents as the necessary effect produced by high wages upon profits
in all branches of industry, is directly contrary to
our experience in each particular trade. Though
it would be going too far to assert, that high
wages and high profits are always co-existent;
yet this proposition would be much nearer to
the truth than that which has been announced
by Mr Ricardo. It is only in very singular circumstances, that wages can possibly advance, while profits are depressed; but when
profits are high, a rise in the wages of the workman may usually be foreseen. A new demand
for a commodity at first enriches those who, being
in possession of this commodity, are enabled to

---

* Ricardo. Principles of Political Economy, chap. 6.

raise its price; the desire to participate in their gains soon directs new capital to its production, and a rise in wages speedily ensues.

This, which may be considered as the usual progress, is the consequence of that principle of the science which teaches, that there is a constant tendency to equalization both of profits and of wages. When a manufacturer becomes desirous of producing an extra quantity of goods, he requires additional capital to enable him to employ more workmen. This he procures in part by a rapid sale of the goods he has on hand, and of those which he successively brings forward to market; the merchant who purchases them being enabled, partly by a quick sale to the consumer, and partly by directing a greater proportion of his stock to this particular article, to replace the manufacturer's capital more expeditiously, and thus to increase its power of defraying the cost of production. Should the demand still exceed the supply, new manufacturers will soon start up, till by competition the profits are reduced. But all this new stock was formerly employed in some other kind of production. It was either advanced by the merchant to some other manufacturer in the purchase of his commodities, or it was vested by its owner in some other trade, or lent out to some other trader. In proportion, therefore, as more of it has been directed to one particular branch of business, less must remain for the others; and therefore the general rate of profit in the country will be somewhat raised.

In like manner, the new demand for labour will advance its price in the prosperous manufacture; and although, by the influx of new workmen, those wages will again decline, other trades from which the workmen have been drawn, will be less fully supplied, and the general rate of wages will be somewhat advanced.

Such will be the effects of increased demand acting first on profits, and, through them, on wages. But in consequence of war, sickness, ot emigration, there may be a considerable rise of wages, without any increase of demand for the produce of labour; and in such circumstances it may be thought that profits must decline.

The proportion that wages bear to the whole capital employed is exceedingly various in the several branches of trade; and as in them all profits tend to equalization, the relative prices of the commodities themselves, in consequence of higher wages, must undergo an alteration. Either those articles which require much labour must rise, or those which require little labour must fall. The additional wages paid for manufacturing a piece of fine lace may be equal to one-fourth of its value, while those paid for some coarse commodity may not exceed one-fiftieth. It is obviously impossible that the former could continue to be produced at all, unless its price were to advance in proportion to its increased cost.

It may be supposed, however, that the price of such articles as are least affected by the advance of wages will fall; and this undoubtedly would be the case, if the capital of the country were as effective in bringing commodities to market after, as before, the advance of wages. On such a supposition, the price that could be afforded for the whole of the commodities offered for sale could not be increased; because the whole revenue of the society, which is the measure of the demand for those commodities, had not been augmented. The relative prices of various articles would be altered, and the production of some might be abandoned; but their aggregate quantity, and the proportion borne by that aggregate quantity to the expenditure of the inhabitants, being unchanged, the value of the whole commodities could not be advanced.

This supposition, however, is very far from the truth. The capital that could have brought to market one hundred pieces of goods, will be unable, after the rise of wages, to produce in one branch more than eighty, in another perhaps ninety-five. While the demand continues the same, and the distribution of capital unaltered, the deficiency of supply in each will be exactly proportioned to the degree in which the manufactures have been respectively affected by the rise of wages; and thus, while their relative prices are entirely altered, that of both will be advanced.

So long as the same capital remains vested in the same trades, a rise of wages will thus occasion a total derangement in the usual comparative prices of various kinds of goods. Imported goods, as they may be brought to market in the usual quantity, will not be enhanced; coarse manufactures, in which wages are a small part of the cost, will be little advanced; while articles of expensive manufacture, being produced in greatly diminished quantity, may rise to a most extravagant price. This will happen whenever the article is such, that those accustomed to its use are extremely unwilling to relinquish its enjoyment. In this case, a competition may arise among purchasers, all eager to acquire it, which will raise its price much higher than is necessary to compensate the additional wages; until such time as high profits allure additional stock from other employments, to make up the deficiency in the quantity of the article offered for sale, and thus to render the supply again equal to the demand.

The more usual effect will be, that the demand for those goods, of which the price is most enhanced, will decline more than their supply, and that the dealers in them will be unable for a time to procure an adequate profit. But if the general expenditure of the country be not diminished, this will derange, only for a short time, the equality among the several employments of stock; and as the whole capital, after the rise of wages, can bring fewer goods to market, while the general demand is undiminished, there will be a rise in the price of the whole of those goods equal to the deficiency of supply, that is, to the rise of wages, in whatever proportion that rise may affect the various commodities that are offered for sale.

On this subject, it appears to me that Mr Malthus has been led, by his own doctrines regarding population, to concede a great deal too much to Mr Ricardo*. Whether in a country of limited territory, without means of drawing subsistence from abroad, and with a population pressing so hard on the means of subsistence, that every rise in the price of the necessaries of life must occasion an immediate rise of wages, or immediate depopulation; whether in such circumstances, the rate of profit must continue necessarily to fall, till the accumulation of capital shall cease, I apprehend it is of extremely little importance to inquire. Such a state of matters bears no resemblance to any thing of

---

* Principles of Political Economy, chap. 5. sect. 1.

which we have experience, and reasonings founded upon its assumption are quite inapplicable to the affairs of the world. Until the people be reduced to a state of such misery, that the slightest deterioration of their condition must necessarily diminish their numbers, I have endeavoured to shew that the price of the necessaries of life has no influence whatever on the rate of wages; and while the general expenditure of the nation remains undiminished, that a rise of wages has no influence whatever on the rate of profit. If I am right in those positions, there is no necessary tendency, in the progress of society, to a point at which capital, in consequence of the rise of wages, ceases to yield profit, and therefore to increase.

It is true, as has been fully illustrated by Dr Smith*, that as wealth increases, wages usually advance, and profits usually decline; capital

---

* Wealth of Nations, Book I. chap. 8. and 9.

being accumulated more rapidly than population increases on the one hand, or expenditure on the other.

Independently of the settlement of foreigners in the country, which seldom takes place to any considerable extent, population must always lag behind an increasing demand. The funds for the maintenance of labour advance by annual accumulation; the number of labourers increase only as marriages, in consequence of this new encouragement, become more frequent, and as the children of those marriages approach to manhood. The demand for labour in a prosperous country has therefore a tendency to outstrip the supply, and allowances being made for temporary fluctuations, the circumstances of the labouring classes are gradually improved.

Where accumulation of stock is rapid, it also, in some degree, outstrips the demand for the new commodities which it annually brings to market. Indeed it is only by saving from revenue, by national consumption falling short of national production, that wealth can accumulate at all ; and though the greater part of this saving be very speedily consumed by the labourers to whom it is paid as wages, part of it also is vested in machinery, and in an additional stock of raw materials or manufactured goods, without adding directly to the general expenditure. From year to year, capital, thus increasing somewhat faster than the expenditure of the society, and consequently than the demand for its products, is forced to seek out new employments for itself at home or abroad, and in many cases, that it may not remain idle, to engage in speculations of which the profits are somewhat inferior to what might formerly be considered as the usual rate.

These are the natural consequences of the admitted principles of supply and demand ; and they account sufficiently for the advance of wages and decline of profits which Dr Smith has remarked as the usual indications of in-

creasing wealth. If by them the facts are sa-
tisfactorily explained, there is no reason to in-
fer, that the rates of wages and of profits are
necessarily connected with each other, as cause
and effect; or that the fluctuations of the one
are necessarily in the inverse ratio of those of
the other.

That in possible cases there may be a limit
to the accumulation of capital, from the difficulty of putting it to any profitable use, it might
be rash to deny; but this is rather an ideal limit,
than one of which we have any actual knowledge or experience. Should capital find no profitable employment in one country, it will soon go
to seek for it in another, either in the shape of
loans to foreign states and foreign merchants,
or much more generally, though less perceptibly, by an extension of credit on goods
sold abroad. When little is to be made of money at home, there will be less objection to indulge a foreign correspondent with an extension of the usual term of credit; to pay foreign-

ers for goods on proper security before their de-livery, or perhaps even before their production; and to engage in distant speculations, of which the returns may not be received for several years. There is, therefore, some tendency to diffusion of capital, not only among the several branches of trade carried on in the same coun-try, but also, though in a less degree, among all the nations of the globe. This tendency is no doubt checked by the risks attending foreign investments; but risks will be run rather than wealth should be allowed to remain unproduc-tive; and therefore capital will not lose its uses anywhere, till every corner of the world has ac-quired as large a share of it as can be produc-tively employed. A limit such as this may safely be disregarded in political science.

Even this limit Mr Say*, Mr Ricardo†,

---

* Traite d'Econ. Pol. Liv. I. Ch. 15. and Lettres a M. Malthus.

† Principles of Political Economy, chap. 21.

and several other authors, will not admit, being of opinion, that capital in every case occasions a demand for its own produce. In reference to the whole commercial world, except perhaps in very singular circumstances, their opinion seems to be correct. The wealth that is saved from expenditure is immediately employed as capital in agriculture, manufactures, or commerce. Being consumed in order to be reproduced with a profit, it causes a demand for some commodities, though perhaps for very different commodities from those which it would have brought into demand had it been expended for the gratification of its proprietor. It is distributed to labourers, to mechanics, to sailors, by whom it is expended on food or clothes for their own consumption; or, being employed in purchasing goods to be carried to remote countries, it replaces the capital of farmers or manufacturers more quickly, and consequently enables those capitals to be more frequently consumed and reproduced. Money saved therefore, unless it be fixed in machinery, is not withdrawn from consumption, but merely expended in a different manner, and its value being reproduced, is consumed after every reproduction, in place of creating only a single demand for commodities, as would have been the case if it had been devoted to the gratification of its owner. Its profit too, if not spent, is added to the capital; in either way creating a new demand for the produce of land, capital, and labour *.

But confining our attention to a single country, it is not so certain that capital will always occasion a demand for its own productions. Had the revenue been spent, it would, in a great degree, have gone to the purchase of home made goods. But if, from circumstances formerly noticed, profits should be lower at home than abroad, it may be lent to foreign merchants or foreign governments, and thus be altogether withdrawn from the country; or it

---

* See on this subject, Lettres a M. Malthus, par M. Say.

may be vested in a distant carrying trade, without producing any demand whatever for commodities at home. As capital, it may create a demand for the productions of China or Japan; as expenditure, it would have given encouragement, at least in a great proportion, to native industry.

It is then conceivable, that by parsimony, in particular circumstances, some encouragement may be taken from native industry, and that a very rapid accumulation of wealth may still farther reduce the rate of profit, when it is already much depressed. But this is neither very likely to occur, nor, if it should be observable in a slight degree, is it without advantages, by which it is perhaps compensated. While the capitalist remains in the country, a portion of the profits derived from his trade will probably be spent, and thus from year to year increase the demand for home commodities; and if any revolution take place in trade, or if a war be entered into, the capital itself will be recalled, to add to the productive wealth of the country, or to furnish war supplies, which otherwise must have been a deduction from that wealth.

A very opposite opinion from that which we have now been considering, has been adopted by the French economists *, by Lord Lauderdale †, and in some degree by Mr Malthus ‡. These authors seem to think it not only possible, but by no means improbable, that parsimony may be carried so far as to check the consumption of goods, and render their production useless. No apprehension can have less foundation; for even if it were conceivable that in any nation the desire for accumulation should so entirely overcome all the other desires of the human heart, this strange and anomalous feeling could not extend over neighbouring coun-

---

* Physiocratie Ire. partie Max. Gen.

† Inquiry into the Nature and Origin of Public Wealth, chap. 4.

‡ Principles of Political Economy, chap. 7. sect. 3 and 9.

tries, whose consumption would increase, as
the commodities furnished by this singularly
parsimonious people fell in price. The consequences of a very large increase of capital by
parsimony, would be to raise the rate of wages,
and, in a still greater degree, to lower that of
profits. The first would enable the people to
live better, or to contract earlier marriages;
and, therefore, unless the mania reached even to
the lowest orders, the demand for articles of
consumption would in so far be restored. The
reduction of the rate of profit, notwithstanding
the rise of wages, would occasion a fall in the
price of goods, every capitalist being willing to
take a small return for his capital, rather than
leave it unemployed. Hence, even with
diminished expenditure, a demand would arise
at home, from the reduced rates, for a pro-
portionally greater quantity of goods; and
should we conceive that this very parsimonious people would see in this cheapness of all
commodities only a farther possibility of ac-

cumulation, foreign countries, free from the
contagion, would increase their demands, till the
surplus produce were diffused over the world;
and perhaps the introduction of new luxuries
from abroad might at last undermine that extraordinary covetousness by which the glut in the
home market had been produced.

But I have been reasoning against strange
and wild suppositions, which have no foundation in human nature. Some accumulate wealth,
others squander it away; and though the proportion between these classes varies somewhat
at different times and in different countries, the
variations are only within moderate limits.
Where property, besides being secure, leads to
power or consideration, accumulation will be
more rapid than in countries in which all honour
is confined to birth, and where extravagance,
instead of being punished by poverty, is the
road to favour, and perhaps to power: and although, when riches are held in too great esti-

mation, the high and virtuous feelings of a people may be lowered, I believe it would be difficult to point out any instance in which parsimony has put an end to, or even much impaired, the productive powers of wealth.

Holland is the only country in ancient or modern times, that has been referred to as approaching to that condition in which capital yielded what we are apt to think an inadequate profit. But the territory of that singular country is so limited, and was so highly cultivated at an early period, that every employment of new stock in agriculture has long been precluded. Its commerce was in a great measure a carrying trade, which was necessarily abridged as other nations acquired sufficient capital to carry on their own exchanges. The habits of the Dutch, too, were parsimonious beyond what has been recorded of those of any other nation. If it were possible for accumulation to be pushed so far as to destroy every motive to farther parsimony, it is to Holland certainly that we must look for such an effect. But previously to the late invasion by the French, though commerce is said to have decreased*, there was no appearance of poverty among the people, such as will ever attend a decay of wealth ; the desire of accumulation seemed to have suffered no check among the rich, and was even extended to those classes which elsewhere would have been denominated the poor ; and the rate of interest being about $2\frac{1}{2}$ or 3 per cent., while in England it was 4, showed that profits, though reduced, were still very far from being annihilated.

It may be granted that merchants and manufacturers, from their daily experience of the advantages to be derived from capital, are generally more economical than other classes. But they are not so very penurious a race as Mr Mal-

---

* Dr Smith states some reasons for discrediting even this conjecture. Wealth of Nations, Book I. chap. 9.

thus seems to imagine; and it is much to be feared, that in this country at least, their economical habits have been considerably injured by the hazardous, and occasionally very lucrative, speculations to which, during the war, they became habituated. In comparison with the prizes in the great lottery in which they were engaged, the fruits of economy seemed unworthy of regard, and a very general taste prevailed for luxuries and splendour, which some years before would have been thought unsuitable to their fortunes. But even were our merchants to revert to the economical habits of former times, their parsimony would not surely be very formidable to the state, while landholders, capitalists, and the great body of the people, continued to live, as it is to be feared they will too generally, to the full extent of their incomes.

Even if there were danger of parsimony being carried too far, and if any possible evil could ensue, I should hesitate before I could join Mr Malthus in recommending that a class of consumers should be supported by taxes, for the purpose of maintaining an effective demand for our goods *. If such be not Mr Malthus' meaning, he has expressed himself unfortunately; for there neither is, nor has been, any question about confining, by public regulations, the numbers or incomes of those classes of the inhabitants, who, though denominated unproductive by Dr Smith and Mr Malthus, return as fair a compensation for their wages as any other description of labourers. The sole question is, whether, with the view of encouraging production, useless stipendiaries should be maintained by the state.

Because, according to a distinction nearly abandoned, but which Mr Malthus has endea-

---

* Principles of Political Economy, chap. 7. sect. 9.

voured to revive*, those who confer upon us the greatest delight and the most important benefits, though they produce no tangible commodity, are classed with public stipendiaries, from whose services neither pleasure nor advantage results, Mr Malthus draws the same conclusion with regard to them all. But physicians, lawyers, authors, actors, musicians, menial servants, and many other of Dr Smith's unproductive labourers, give to their employers a full equivalent for what they receive from them; of which no better proof can be desired than the willingness of the one party to exchange their goods or money for the services of the other.

---

* Principles of Political Economy, chap. 1. sect. 2.

In another publication I have stated my reasons for rejecting this distinction. Elements of Political Science, Book II. chap. 4. sect. 3. What I have there stated I see no reason to alter. I have admitted the existence of an abstract distinction between labour that necessarily perishes in an instant, and labour that may be stored up in commodities; but I have denied both the accuracy of this distinction, as the terms productive and unproductive have been employed, and its usefulness in Political Economy.

Public officers, also, in the peace, security, and prosperity of the state, give the most ample compensation for the salaries which they receive. But public stipendiaries who do no public service, whether sinecurists, or useless soldiers, sailors, diplomatists, or clerks, deprive every citizen of part of his income without any equivalent; and if maintained by the state for the purpose of increasing expenditure, and, through it, demand, as seems to be recommended by Mr Malthus, they give precisely that kind of encouragement to industry and enterprize, that would be afforded to a shop-keeper whose trade was not very brisk, by burning part of his goods before his door, without paying him their price.

— — —

CHAPTER IV.

OF RENT.

IF a person, who employs his own labour on his own land, reap more corn than he had sown, the surplus, after replacing his food, is partly profit on the capital from which he had advanced his own maintenance, and partly rent arising from the nature of the soil. When he employs servants, horses, and a variety of implements, to cultivate more land, and to cultivate it better, all the crop that remains, after replacing the maintenance and wages of himself and his servants, the food of his horses, and the repairs of his implements, is, in like manner, profit on his capital, or rent derived from what may properly be called the productive services of his land. The two are indeed confounded together, all that he knows or cares about being that his barns are fuller after each harvest, than if he had retained in them the corn that he issued during the year as seed, maintenance, and wages.

But as soon as his servants are rich enough to maintain themselves and their cattle, though not to stock their farms, they agree with the landlord to give him a proportion of the crop for the use of the land, the cattle, and the implements; and under this tenure, the wages are entirely detached from the rent, though neither of them is completely separated from the profit of stock. Part of what the farmer receives of the crop is the wages or maintenance of himself, his assistants, and his cattle; but part also is profit on that fund of previously acquired wealth, from which he was able to make the necessary advances of that maintenance. The landlord's proportion, in like manner, is partly profit on the farming stock and implements which he had contributed to the joint undertaking, and partly rent for the equally essential implement of production, the land.

At last the farmer, having acquired sufficient capital to stock the farm, is independent of the landlord for every thing but the use of the land, without which he is unable to proceed. He is still therefore forced to offer part of the produce, or a fixed annual sum, as a compensation for those services of the land which he has no other means of procuring; and rents are then completely detached both from wages and profits*.

---

* To speak more accurately, part of the rent paid to the landlord is still profit on the fixed capital vested in the houses on the farm, as noticed by Mr Ricardo. But I shall soon have occasion to shew, that the profit of fixed capital is very much of the same nature with rent.

The nature of rent, however, is not changed by being thus detached. It is still that part of the produce which is owing to the fertility of the soil, though it may no longer be paid to the landlord in that produce, but in money. It is the extra production of the capital and labour, beyond what they would have returned, had they been employed in any way in which, without the assistance of land, they might have been productive ; and that it is an extra production is clear from this circumstance, that the farmer is willing to resign it to the landlord, rather than remove his capital to what he knows would be a less productive employment. The land yielding as real a service as the labourer or the farming stock, its proprietor is as fairly entitled to his share of the crop.

If it be asked, in what way the proportion that ought to belong to the landlord is to be ascertained, the answer is obvious ; by that competition which alone fixes and determines every kind of value. The landlord is desirous to get as much as he can, the tenant to give him as little rent as circumstances will permit; and the rent that will finally be fixed by their higgling, must be that proportion of the crop which remains, after restoring all the annual outlay on the farm, together with such a profit on the farmer's capital as it probably might have yielded in other employments. Much more than this the tenant will not give, while other trades are open to him; and much less than this the landlord will not accept, knowing that should his tenant quit the farm, a slight prospect of advantage will speedily draw new capital to his land from other investments. If too low a rent be fixed, the farmer will either from indolence fail in producing that value which ought to have paid part of the rent, or he will appropriate to himself a portion of the crop, which, being properly the produce of the land, ought to have belonged to the landlord. If the rent be too high, the landlord will draw more of the general produce than has resulted from the services of his land, and the farmer will have less than the ordinary rate of profit on his capital. In neither case, unless the annual produce be diminished by slovenly culture, will the market price of the crop, or its aggregate value, be in the least degree affected by the terms of the lease. That is a matter which concerns only the contracting parties, the one of whom may be enriched at the expence of the other, but is altogether immaterial to the rest of the community. If we could conceive rents to be totally abolished, those farmers who were so fortunate as to get possession of land without paying for it, would pocket what ought to have gone to the landlord, and the price of corn would remain unchanged. If, on the other hand, we should suppose rents to be raised extravagantly, the tenant would be gradually impoverished; for he could not, in consequence of his imprudent bargain, add one farthing to the price or value of the crop.

Rent, then, is that portion of the produce of land which remains, after having replaced the whole produce that had been expended on the farming operations, besides returning a profit on the farming stock equal to what a capital of the same amount would have gained, during an equal period, in manufactures or commerce.

This surplus is independent of barter or of price, and must furnish rent to some person whenever, by means of agricultural processes, or rearing of cattle, more produce comes annually into the possession of the farmer than he could have acquired by employing his accumulated stock of provisions and clothing, in the purchase of the raw material of a manufacture, and in the maintenance of those persons and their families by whom its form was to be improved.

To this simple, and, as it appears to me, very satisfactory, account of the nature of rent, Mr Malthus has added two other circumstances, by which the idea is in my apprehension obscured. He has ascribed the existence of rent in part to

" that quality," which he conceives to be " pe-
" culiar to the necessaries of life, of being able,
" when properly distributed, to create their own
" demand, or to raise up a number of demand-
" ers, in proportion to the quantity of necessaries
" produced." And he has farther ascribed it
" to the comparative scarcity of fertile land,
" either natural or artificial*."

These circumstances may perhaps tend to
account for the actual rental of this, or
any other country; but they seem to have no
connection with the inquiry into the abstract
nature of rent. It is even doubtful whether
the produce of land, more than that of capital,
has a tendency to create a demand for itself.
Unless there be increasing employment for labourers, and consequently a progressive improvement in their general condition, the
people will not increase their numbers merely

---

* Principles of Political Economy, chap. 3. sect. 1.—See also
his Inquiry into the Nature and Progress of Rent.

because they may be fed, more than because they may be lodged, or clothed, or amused ; and while any valuable article, however useless it may be for subsistence, is produced in a country enjoying intercourse with the rest of the world, a demand will be found for that article just as certainly as for food. A new machine making hats for fifty people, or for a thousand, would create demand by low prices, just as readily as a new field, which yielded an extra quantity of provisions for the same number of persons. If there be any difference, it is probably in favour of the machine; both because people are more easily induced to wear better hats, than to increase the quantity of their ordinary food, and from the superior facility of transporting manufactures to every corner of the world. When every man indeed had got as many hats as he wanted, and even long before this, the demand would be so much reduced, that new capital, when acquired, would be employed in producing any other commodity rather than hats; and exactly in the same manner, long before every man in the world had as much corn as he could wish for, landholders and farmers would find it more profitable to raise timber, flax, hemp, wool, or fruit, than grain. But even allowing Mr Malthus' position to be true, it would still be incontrovertible, that the rent was the surplus produce after paying wages and profit, though it might follow that that surplus produce was more valuable, or in more permanent demand, than if it had consisted in other articles than those used as food.

The same remark applies to Mr Malthus' other observation. The greater scarcity there is of fertile land, its produce is likely to be more valuable; but unless land were so plenty that, like air or water, every one might have as much of it as he could employ, its surplus produce would be of some value, and consequently the landholder would receive some rent.

The doctrine of the French economists, therefore, is just, although they drew from it many erroneous conclusions * ; and in endeavouring to strengthen it by extraneous views, I fear **Mr** Malthus has only rendered it more obscure and perplexed. But other modern authors seem on this subject to have fallen into much greater and more serious errors.

Following some detached expressions, rather than considered opinions, of **Dr** Smith, several authors have ascribed rent entirely to monopoly, representing the revenue of the landlord, if not a robbery of the other inhabitants, at least as a

---

* Mr Malthus, in his *Inquiry into the Nature and Progress of Rent*, ranks the French economists among those who have ascribed the existence of rent to monopoly. It rather appears to me, that this ingenious sect viewed it in its proper light, as an additional production of the land itself, beyond the wages and profits of the farmer ; and that it was by an erroneous inference from this sound doctrine, that they were led to represent it as the only disposable revenue of the nation, and consequently as the fund from which every description of tax must ultimately be drawn.

deduction from their incomes; a charge on all, created for the benefit of a few*.

It cannot indeed, be denied, that if every man could procure as much land as he wished to occupy, there could be neither rent nor value of land; and on such a supposition, Political Economy would have as little reference to land, as to the light of the sun. But this is equally true of labour and of capital, the value of which would be annihilated the moment their quantity became unlimited. Who, that could command labour by a wish, would pay the wages of a workman? Who, that could conjure up all the capital he could employ, would pay interest for a loan? To assign the origin of rent to monopoly, in this sense of the word, is not therefore to explain what is peculiar in its

---

* It is to be regretted that Mr Say should have used any expression which may be understood as acquiescing in an opinion that the tenor of his reasonings tends to refute. Traité d'Ec. Pol. Liv. II. chap. 9.

nature, but merely to assert a truism, which does not even touch on those circumstances, from which a landholder, without diminishing the wealth of others, or the gratification which they may derive from a similar property in their limbs, their machinery, or their commodities, is enabled to draw a revenue from his land. What knowledge should we gain by being told that all value was the consequence of monopoly, or, in other words, of the impossibility of commanding every enjoyment by a wish? Yet this seems to be the amount of a doctrine which has been considered as a satisfactory account of the nature of rent, by several men of undoubted talents. If land yielded no surplus produce, [*produit net*] its monopoly, however strict, could create no rent ; and if it does yield such a surplus, after defraying the charges of cultivation, and the ordinary rate of profit on the farmer's stock, this is the rent, whether it be enjoyed by the farmer in consequence of an advantageous lease, or by the proprietor, or, if land were held in common, by the community.

Mr Ricardo* has proposed a new theory of rent, which, in as far as it is just, is equally a truism with that opinion which ascribes it to monopoly. According to him, rent arises entirely from the circumstance of land of various qualities being in use at the same time. The worst land produces only such a crop as will repay the cost of tillage, and the farmer's profit. Better lands produce more than this in various degrees; and as the profits of all farmers are reduced by competition to one level, there is a surplus produce from superior lands, according to their degree of fertility, which is detached from the profit, and constitutes the rent. In every country the best soils are first cultivated; and as they yield equal returns, corn at this time will be cheap, and no rent whatever will accrue to the proprietor. But as population increases, it becomes necessary to have recourse to land of inferior quality, which, however, must return the cost and profit of

---

* Principles of Political Economy, chap. 2.

cultivation. As the fertile soils give larger crops at the same expence, there appears a surplus produce from them above what is derived from the inferior lands, and this surplus now constitutes a rent to their proprietors. By degrees recourse is had to soils of a third, a fourth, and a fifth quality, and at every such time, as the worst land must pay the cost and profit, the rent of the more fertile is necessarily advanced.

This opinion may be so understood as to be perfectly correct; but in this sense it is merely a new way of expressing an old and established doctrine. If rent be the surplus produce after paying outlay and profit, as seems to be very generally admitted, it must of necessity be the same with the surplus produce above that yielded by lands, whether existing or imaginary, that produce nothing whatever beyond that outlay and profit. The two propositions, when understood, are clearly identical; and all that the new theory has done is to dress up a received opinion in new phraseology.

I am aware that identical propositions, by presenting different aspects of the same truth, may sometimes usher the way to important discoveries; but I confess, when old opinions appear in new language, experience leads me to anticipate perplexity and error, rather than truth; and I cannot help thinking that the opinions of Mr Ricardo, with regard to rent, form no exception to the general rule.

Having established superiority of fertility above the worst lands in culture, as the measure of rent, Mr Ricardo infers that the resorting to inferior soils, or less profitable modes of cultivation, is the sole and efficient cause of a rise in rents, and the abandoning of inferior soils the sole and efficient cause of their decline. In the one case, the difference between the best and worst lands in tillage, which is the measure of rent, is increased; in the other case, that difference is diminished.

That this is an inaccurate view of the subject, will, I think, be apparent, by putting a possible, though not a very probable, case. Let us suppose all the lands of a kingdom to be already cultivated, and importation of corn prohibited; while, from skill in manufactures, and habits of economy, the capital and population are rapidly increased. In such circumstances, the demand for agricultural produce, and consequently its value, may be extravagantly heightened, till such time as the farther increase of population is stopped by the physical impossibility of finding subsistence. Long before this takes place, the annual returns from the land will be prodigiously raised in value, without any necessary, or even probable, advance, either in the expenses of culture, which depend on the rate of wages fixed by other causes, or on the farmer's profit, which depends on that yielded by other descriptions of capital. Even from the worst land there will gradually arise a great surplus produce, which, at the expiry of each current lease, will be detached from the farmer's profit, and made over to the landholder; and a high rent being thus drawn even from the poorest lands, the difference between the best and worst soils under culture, though it will still measure their relative, will cease to measure their absolute, rents.

To render tenable the theory which we are reviewing, two assumptions seem to be necessary:— 1*st*, That in every country there is indefinitely a regular gradation of lands, from the most fertile to the most barren, or a regular gradation of cultivation, from the most to the least productive; and 2*dly*, That in each step of this gradation, there is a sufficiency of land fully to supply the increased demand. If the gradation be not regular, the price of agricultural produce may rise considerably, and along with it the general rate of rent, without calling into use those soils which, notwithstanding this rise in the value of produce, it may not yet be possible to cultivate to advantage. At every such time, the worst lands will yield a rent, contrary to the theory, till new lands can be profitably broken up. If, again, the quantity of new land that can be brought into culture be of small extent, it can have so trifling an effect, that it must appear very unsatisfactory to ascribe to such a cause the general rise of rents over an extensive kingdom. It is well known, that during the melting of ice, the whole water by which it is surrounded, remains steadily at the freezing point; but who ever concluded from this, that the temperature of the sea could be reduced to 32 degrees, even for an instant, by tossing a piece of ice into the ocean?

Indeed there seems no reason to conclude that either of those assumptions is founded on fact. Land unfit for the plough may feed cattle, or sheep, or goats, or roebuck, or grouse; or it may raise timber or firewood; or it may be cut for turf; and in one or other of these ways, it yields to its proprietor some, though perhaps a very small rent, either in money, or in what he values as highly, in sport. It may be doubted therefore, whether, in a well peopled country, Mr Ricardo's standard will be any where to be found.

It may be still farther doubted, whether of those lands yielding no rent, there be regular gradations, such as will ensure successive improvement, in proportion as the demand for produce increases; and whether of each description there be that quantity, which, by its culture, can supply the increasing demand. If there be not, there must evidently occur stages in the progress, at which the last cultivated lands will yield rent, without its being profitable to inclose or till as much of inferior quality as can affect the price of food.

It is true, that a rise of rent is in general very speedily followed by the improvement of new land, and superior culture of the old. If, on this account, the one of these results must be considered as the cause of the other, Mr Ricardo seems to have been singularly unfortunate in his choice. Till the lowest quality of land in culture yield some rent, and even a considerable rent, there can be little inducement to take in more land of worse quality, which in such circumstances is not likely to repay the cost of improvement. Rise of rent will therefore be prior in time to new cultivation; and I know no system of logic in which that which is confessedly the last in the sequence, is considered as the cause of what uniformly precedes it*.

---

* " It follows, therefore," says Mr Malthus, in his *Inquiry into the Nature and Progress of Rent*, " that it can never answer to take fresh lands of a poorer quality into cultivation, " till rents have risen, or would allow of a rise, on what is already cultivated."

And again, " It appears then that the power of extending " cultivation and increasing produce, both by the cultivation " of fresh land and the improvement of the old, depends entirely upon the existence of such prices compared with the " expense of production, as would raise rents in the actual " state of cultivation."

Both, in truth, are consequences of a rise in the price of agricultural produce occasioned by an increased demand. This rise of price adds, in the first instance, to the profits of the farmer; at the end of his lease, it passes to the landlord under the form of advanced rent; and the same demand, by holding out the prospect of profit from agricultural speculations, allures additional capital to be employed either in reclaiming wastes, or in cultivating more effectually those lands already improved. Both the rise of rent, and the extended cultivation, being thus the natural results of that great principle of the science by which all wages, all profits, and all rents, are regulated, and by which capital is distributed among the several employments useful to mankind, it is unnecessary to consider two nearly simultaneous consequences of the same state of the country as related to each other by causation, and particularly unphilosophical to designate as the cause, that which is generally, if not universally, of latest occurrence.

It evidently follows, from the nature of rent, as it has now been explained, that whatever raises the expense of cultivation, whether it be an advance of wages and of the ordinary profits of stock, or a tax on horses and on implements used in agriculture, must diminish rents; and that whatever lowers the expense of cultivation must increase them. The landlord's share, being all of the produce that remains after paying the annual outlay with a profit proportioned to that derived from other employments of capital, must vary according to the degree in which the value of the whole produce exceeds the cost of production. If the crop be the same, the rent will be affected in an inverse ratio, by every thing that increases or diminishes the necessary expenses of the farm.

Between the profits of fixed capital and the rent of land, there is so close an analogy, that, in a former work, I was led to consider them as entirely similar in their nature, as well as in the laws by which they are governed*. Both consist of the portion of gross produce that remains, after defraying the wages of labour, and the usual profits of the circulating capital, without the employment of which there could neither be rent for the land nor profit on the machine. If this excess be large, more capital becomes fixed in new machinery, or in clearing, draining, and inclosing waste lands. If it be small, the profits of the fixed capital, or the rent of the estate, is of little amount. If it be reduced to nothing, the machines are laid aside, and the land is allowed to run to waste.

So much do those sources of revenue resemble each other, that even in ordinary language the return for fixed capital, when the necessary circulating capital is supplied by a different person, is always denominated its rent. Yet, on a more accurate view, some differences

---

* Elements of Political Science, Book. II. chap. 4. sect. 2.

between them will be apparent, which it might be unsafe to disregard.

1st, Machines can be multiplied to any extent required by the demand, and those last erected will be as productive as the first; while the quantity of land is limited by nature, and, after a certain degree of amelioration, the employment of a greater amount of capital on a farm yields a smaller proportional return. In consequence of this, fixed capital cannot continue in any circumstances to yield much more profit than is usually drawn from the employment of circulating capital, without multiplying the machines till the extra profit disappears; while in a very prosperous state of a country already fully cultivated, if importation of corn be prohibited, there is scarcely any assignable limit to the advance of the rent.

2dly, If the demand for a commodity decline so far, that the whole produce of the machinery employed in its manufacture is absorbed by the

wages and the profit of the circulating capital,
the fixed capital, as nothing will remain for its
profit, has entirely lost its value, and can no
longer be considered as part of either private or
public wealth. But although land, in similar
circumstances, may be thrown out of culture, it
never loses its value entirely, but by feeding
some cattle, or raising some timber, it will always yield to its proprietor some kind of revenue. This indeed for a time may be extremely
small; but the cheapness of provisions by which
it has been lowered having a tendency to increase the demand, the rent after some years
may be expected again to improve. The returns from fixed capital are entirely dependent
on the co-operation of circulating stock: diminish the latter, and in a greater degree you reduce
the value of the former: withdraw the one,
and you annihilate the other. But land will
always, in one way or other, produce something
beyond the profit of the circulating capital employed upon it, which excess, however small,

can scarcely in any circumstances cease to exist. A field, twenty acres of which will feed only a single cow or a few sheep, has still a value and rent proportional to this return.

3dly, The invention of better machinery annihilates the value of all that has been erected on an inferior principle; because the superior may be multiplied (and, if profitable, will be multiplied) to such an extent, as fully to supply the demand at a price insufficient to defray the annual charges of ill constructed machines. But superior culture, although, where adopted, it may yield higher profits to the farmer, and advanced rents to the landlord, will, in a very slight degree, if at all, reduce the rents of other lands. For a short time, the additional produce may tend to lower the price of food; but the increased consumption consequent on cheapness will soon bring the demand nearly to the supply.

4thly, The most important distinction, however, between machinery and land is, that the former is gradually deteriorated by use, while the latter is gradually improved. A machine is in its best state when newly erected, and, however carefully repaired, at last becomes unserviceable; at which time the capital originally vested in it is lost. But when a field is taken into culture, besides yielding an annual profit on the capital employed in improvement, and repaying all the outlay in a reasonable time, it remains ever after in superior condition, capable of producing more ample returns for the labour and capital annually employed, and therefore of paying an additional rent. This is the case in all judicious improvements, whether by landlord or tenant; but it is most obvious with regard to the latter. Unless the tenant got back, during his lease, what he laid out upon the land, with a fair profit, he could have no inducement to take in a waste field, or to adopt, on his farm, a more efficient, though more expensive, system of cultivation. But the field which he has drained, inclosed, and freed from briars, is by these operations permanently improved, and, being fitted for valuable crops, will let, at the end of the lease, .for an advanced rent. Had his capital been employed in manufactures or trade, he might have enjoyed as high an annual profit; but the permanent revenue which he has bestowed on his landlord, and the permanent addition which he has thus made to the annual produce of the country, would have had no existence. In this respect it cannot be denied that agriculture possesses a decided advantage over every other employment of stock; though this material circumstance seems entirely to have escaped the observation of those late writers, who, in opposition to the opinions of older times, deny the claims of agriculture to any peculiar favour or encouragement from the state.

In examining the effects of taxes levied upon land, it must immediately occur, that, as they cannot in any way increase the demand for agricultural productions, they cannot, unless by diminishing their quantity, have the slightest tendency to raise their price; and it must be equally obvious, that if a contribution be paid to the state without prices being raised, that contribution must entirely fall on one or all of the classes who derive their income from the commodity that is taxed. But the wages of agricultural labour, and the profits of farming capital, are regulated by the rates of other wages, and of other profits; and therefore such taxes solely affect landholders, the only other class of inhabitants who have property in the produce of the soil.

If the tax be laid on only one or a few descriptions of produce, it will indeed diminish their cultivation, and consequently raise their price. But the land formerly employed in growing those crops, in place of being totally abandoned, will immediately be turned to some other branch of farming, and thus, those products of land that remain untaxed being brought to market in greater quantity, their price will be depressed. Whatever variation may take place in the relative quantity and relative price of corn, butcher meat, flax, and timber, the total produce from the land being undiminished, its general price will not be enhanced; and if a tax be levied, without any corresponding advance of price on the one hand, or decline of wages and profit on the other, it must be altogether a deduction from the rent of the landlord.

This truth is still more evident, if we suppose that all the various products of land are equally affected by the tax: for in this case, there being no motive to substitute one kind of production for another, or to change in any respect the established rotation of crops, the usual quantity of each article will be offered for sale, and the demand not having increased, the price of each kind of agricultural produce will remain unvaried.

Every species of land tax, therefore, whether

levied as in England by a permanent valuation, or, as proposed by the French economists, according to the real rent, must be radically and incurably unjust; for it throws upon one class of the inhabitants a charge which, being incurred for the general good, ought equally to affect every kind of wealth. But even this is only a part of its injustice, as it loads with the whole burden of the tax for ever, those unfortunate persons who happen to be landed proprietors at the moment of its imposition. He who buys an estate next day will pay as much less for the land, as the estimated value of the tax to the end of time; for he exchanges capital unreduced in power of production, and consequently in value, for land, of which a part of the rent, in place of going into his pocket, is in future to be applied to the service of the state*.

---

* This consequence of the imposition of a land-tax is more fully illustrated in Elements of Political Science, Book III. Part i. chap. 2. sect. 1.

Mr Say* has attributed to the land-tax of England a consequence which, if it were real, might in some measure compensate its original injustice. He represents it as holding out, by the exemption of new improvements from the operation of the tax, a most powerful, though at the same time, as he thinks, an unjust, encouragement to agriculture. That in this respect the English land-tax is infinitely preferable to that proposed by the economists, cannot be doubted. The latter, as it rose with the rent, necessarily deprived the farmer of part of those profits which were his only inducement to improve his lands during the currency of his lease, and must have been thus directly hostile to the increase of what that ingenious sect considered as the only real or available revenue of the state. But it is not easy to see how the mere absence of a discouragement can operate as a positive bounty; and the English mode of as-

---

* Traité d'Ec. Pol. Liv. III. chap. 8 sect. 4.

sessing the land-tax goes no farther than to provide that such improvements as may have been made after its imposition, by the application of new capital to the land, shall not be less advantageous to the farmer and to the proprietor, than if no such tax had ever been imposed. Nor is it easy to see how this exemption can in any respect be unjust. It is merely saying to landholders, that, having subjected them to one partial tax, from which all their fellow citizens are free, there is no intention, in consequence of the future amelioration of their estates, to subject them to another.

From Mr Ricardo's particular views of the nature of wages, profit, and rent, he has been led to entertain a less unfavourable opinion of the tithe, or tax on the gross produce of land, than that which has been expressed by most writers on the subject. The tithe, according to him, cannot fall on the rent of the worst quality of land, because such land yields no rent ; nor on the profits of its farmer, or the wages of its labourers, which are regulated by the general rates of the country : it must, therefore, raise the price of produce sufficiently to enable the farmer to continue the cultivation of this description of land ; and, by doing so, it falls first on the consumer, and, by raising his wages, ultimately on all the members of the community, according to their expenditure : the tithe he therefore considers as an equal, though in some other respects an objectionable, tax*.

In examining this question, the first remark that occurs, and its truth is fully admitted by Mr Ricardo, is, that no such rise in the price of produce can take place, while importation is permitted from foreign countries. In such circumstances, according to his views, the lands of inferior quality will be thrown out of cultivation, but the chasm in the supply will immediately be filled up with corn from

---

* Ricardo s Principles of Political Economy and Taxation, chap. 11.

abroad; and prices being thus kept down, the whole amount of the tax must become a charge upon the superior lands. He, therefore, who holds this opinion, must be a decided enemy to a free trade in corn, there being no means to prevent the tithe from being an unjust imposition, except the levying of a countervailing duty on importation, and the paying of an equivalent bounty on exportation. Such duties and bounties could scarcely be objected to on principle, as they would merely replace landholders in their natural situation; but they would be far more prejudicial in their consequences than the present, or any former, corn laws; and indeed they could scarcely fail to occasion frequent famines*. If, then, it be necessary, in order to

---

* This is not the place for a discussion of the justice or policy of our corn laws, of which I have already treated in Elements of Political Science; but I may remark, that duties and bounties equivalent to the tithe, in place of equalizing the prices of corn, the most justifiable motive for the interference of government, would have a very opposite effect.

justify the tithe as a source of revenue either to the church or state, to counteract its effects by such impolitic regulations, the question, in as far as relates to its expediency, may be considered as put to rest.

Let us now trace the effects of a heavy tax on gross produce, when first imposed on a country into which no foreign grain is allowed to enter. The first effect would be the prevention of all expensive culture, except on very fertile

---

Suppose a duty of 10 per cent. to be at all times levied on the importation of corn, and a bounty of 10 per cent. paid on its exportation; this would no doubt be a full compensation to the landholders for the tithe; but when wheat was sold at 50s. a quarter, there would be an inducement of only 5s. to export, and a restriction of only 5s. on importation: corn, therefore, might be poured in from cheaper countries, so as to sink prices already too low. But when wheat rose to 140s., and every motive of humanity and policy should prompt us to relieve the necessities of the poor, there would be a duty of 14s. on its importation, and a bounty of 14s. on sending it out of the country. The duties and bounties would be in the inverse ratio of those which justice and policy might equally sanction.

lands. Every farmer would become desirous to raise the cheapest, not the most productive, crops; for that style of cultivation which used to repay the outlay in the most ample manner, would do so no longer, when the tax rose in amount according to the value of the crop. Still the farmer would endeavour to raise something from his lands, though with the employment of as little labour and stock as he could; and the proprietor, when the lease was out, would take what rent he could get, rather than none. There would therefore be a general decay of agriculture, and more of the lands would be turned to those branches of farming in which, by the employment of less capital and labour, a proportionably less valuable crop would be procured. Little or no land, however, would be entirely abandoned; for where the great original expenses of improvement had already been incurred, it never could be for the interest of the proprietor to allow his fields to go to waste. The tithe would thus affect the several descriptions of rude produce in very different degrees.

Crops which required a great deal of stock and labour would be more sparingly raised, and the price of those kinds of produce would advance; but the lands thrown out of this description of crop would be immediately turned to the raising of inferior grain, or to pasture, and the produce of such lands, being in greater plenty than formerly, would fall.

Upon the whole, the amount of the produce of land under a more imperfect system of cropping would be lessened, and a greater proportion of it would consist of inferior grain. There would therefore be, upon the whole, some degree of rise in the price of raw produce, and the tithe would fall partly on the landholder in the reduction of his rent, and partly on the consumers. The proportion in which it might affect these several descriptions of the inhabitants, would depend on many circumstances, of which the most important would be the general prosperity of the country.

If the country be in a very prosperous state, and the population rapidly increasing, the demand for food will be such as to keep all the lands cultivated in the best manner, and this can be done only by a rise of prices equal to that portion of the tithe which is levied from the returns for the stock and labour. If the whole crop be worth L.16 per acre, and the rent L.4, three-fourths of the tithe may be considered as levied from the returns of the farming stock and labour, and one-fourth from the rent. The price of the corn must therefore be raised twenty-four shillings, to afford the same inducement to high cultivation as formerly; but the remaining eight shillings of tithe will be a deduction from the rent. From this charge the landholder has no means of escape; for to whatever purpose he may apply his land, unless he accept of a lower rent, the same tithe will still pursue him.

In a less prosperous state of the country, the landholder will probably be obliged to pay a much larger proportion of the tax. If the demand for produce be stationary or declining, he is in the same circumstances with the proprietor of machinery which produces goods little in request. To raise the price much, or at all, on the consumer, may be impossible; because in such a case less of the article would be made use of: to lower the profits of the circulating capital, or the wages of the labourers, is at least equally impossible, as they are regulated by the usual rates; and, therefore, the tax in some cases will be altogether, and in other cases chiefly, a deduction from the rent. If the demand for produce be not increasing, there will be no cultivation of new lands independently of the tax; and no supply will be kept back from the market by its imposition; nor will the proprietors of lands already cleared, drained, and inclosed, allow their fields to lie waste, rather than suffer some deduction from their rental. To a certain degree, an inferior style of culture may be adopted, particularly on the worst lands; but there is a limit at which, even with the tithe, this must become disadvantageous both to landlord and tenant. The price of some kinds of produce may therefore rise from defective cultivation occasioned by the tax; but after every allowance is made for this (unless we believe that a great deal of land would be left waste without yielding any produce whatever) the landholder will have to pay a great part, or in some cases the whole, of the tithe. If there be no increased demand, there can be no rise of price, except in consequence of a diminished supply; and if the supply is to be diminished, only by rendering lands that are now valuable, unproductive, I do not see how it can well be denied that this, in as far as it takes place, must be at the expense of the proprietors.

But in whatever proportion the tithe, according to the advancing or declining state of the country, may be divided between the landholder and consumer, it must always be a most unjust source of public revenue.

If it raise the price of raw produce, it affects the poor as consumers, much more severely than the rich; raw produce forming almost the whole of the value of commodities from which are derived the subsistence, and the little comforts and enjoyments of the poor; nor, unless all the reasonings contained in another part of this treatise be erroneous, have labourers any means of raising their wages according to the price of necessaries, and of thus rolling over the charge upon their employers.

Even in the circumstances most favourable to landed proprietors, a part of the tithe is an unjust burden upon them, from which the holders of other descriptions of property are exempt. But this is only a part of the hardship of which they have a right to complain. Whatever opposes the best style of cultivation; still more, whatever prevents the improvement of new lands, deprives the proprietor of that amelioration of his estate which, without any expense to him, must have otherwise resulted from the operations of his tenants; and thus, while it becomes a deduction, and in some cases a very serious deduction, from his actual income, the tax precludes the possibility of his enjoying a more ample revenue at a future time.

To the farmer also, tithes are detrimental, by preventing him from laying out his gradual accumulations of capital, under his own eye, in the manner in which they would be most productive to him; while they operate directly as a deduction, to their full extent, from the just reward of his superior activity, enterprize, and knowledge.

To the country, tithes are still more injurious. If accompanied with countervailing duties and bounties, they may occasion famines, and they certainly will increase those fluctuations in the price of food, which are destructive of the comfort, morals, and industry of the people. If unaccompanied by such duties and bounties, they confessedly fall entirely on one class, the landholders, and are a premium on foreign, at the expense of home, cultivation. If this be guarded against by a general prohibition of importation, they raise the price of provisions in an advancing country, to the oppression of the lower orders of the people; and they sink rents in a stationary country, to the oppression of the landholders; while in both cases they limit the productive employments of capital, and, by discouraging agriculture, are injurious to the most important source of national prosperity and wealth.

Such being my views of the effects of this tax, I am not inclined to retract, or even soften, the assertion, that " tithe is the most iniqui-
" tous imposition that was ever invented by
" rapacity, or submitted to through igno-
" rance."

CHAPTER V.

OF THE COMMERCIAL STATE OF BRITAIN SINCE THE YEAR 1815.

THE commercial distress in which Britain has found herself involved since the conclusion of the late war, has been equally severe and unexpected. For a short time after the termination of former wars, considerable depression was no doubt felt in those branches of industry that had been created, or much enlarged, by the particular demands incident to a state of hostilities. By the reduction of the army and navy, some degree of slackness might be observed in the de-

mand for labour, and some decline in the rate
of wages; while those merchants and manufacturers, who had been accustomed to import or
produce the implements of war, suffered some
loss in transferring their capitals to new employments.   But those embarrassments were to a
small extent, and of short duration.   The re-
newal of mutual intercourse among nations soon
gave fresh activity to commerce; and capital
and industry, having adapted themselves to the
new circumstances of the country, soon passed
that point from which they had partially declined, and, springing forward with renewed vi-
gour, speedily restored the national wealth which
had been somewhat reduced by the war-expenditure.

The last war being unexampled in duration,
extent, and exertion, it might have been expected, when peace at last arrived, that the derangement of what had become the established
course of trade would be greater than had formerly been experienced, and probably of some-

what longer continuance. But there seemed no reason to anticipate so universal a depression of wages and profits, or to such a degree, or for so long a time. Peace, though unpropitious to some individuals, had speedily assumed, on all former occasions, her genuine character of parent of industry and nurse of commerce ; and we were not prepared for her appearance, perhaps for the first time on record, as a demon of destruction.

A phenomenon so singular could not fail to attract the attention of all political economists ; and a desire, if possible, to discover some cure for the evil, has given an unusually deep and general interest to their inquiries. Many theories have accordingly been proposed, all perhaps in some respects just ; but each of them by itself unsatisfactory, and many distorted, that they might serve as engines for attacking or defending the policy of the war, or the measures of administration since the peace. In what I have to offer on this difficult and important subject, I am not aware that I shall bring forward any view that will have novelty to recommend it, far less any specific nostrum from which a speedy recovery may be anticipated; though I hope to correct some misapprehensions that have prevailed, and shall endeavour to combine whatever in the several theories seems to be founded in truth.

The chief circumstances then, by which it has been proposed to account for the present state of the country, .are, 1*st*, The transition from a state of war to a state of peace; 2*dly*, The improvement in the value of the currency of the kingdom; 3*dly*, The destruction of capital by the war-expenditure; and 4*thly*, The inability of the nation to support the load of taxes required to pay the interest of an enormous public debt.

SECTION I.

EFFECTS OF THE TRANSITION FROM WAR TO PEACE.

In order to appreciate the consequences of the late transition from a state of war to a state of peace, it will be necessary to consider the nature and extent of the encouragement to production that arose from hostilities, and the sources from which capital and labour commensurate to the increasing demand were procured. In the whole of this inquiry we must also keep in view the uncommon violence and duration of the struggle, together with such other circumstances as may serve to distinguish it from former wars. To ascribe the present state of the country in a general way, to a transition from war to peace, is vague and unsatisfactory, unless we can show what there is in the present circumstances different from those that formerly characterised such transitions. It is not surely enough to say, that some embarrassment has followed the termination of every war : for that derangement of commercial affairs, under which we have suffered, has little resemblance either in intensity, extent, or duration, to any thing experienced on former occasions.

An increased demand for rude produce must in some degree be the consequence of every war. Soldiers and sailors are much better fed on service, than labourers at home; a great number of horses must be reared and kept in good condition for cavalry and for transport; crops to a great extent are sometimes trodden down during a campaign; and all kinds of provisions are always wasted through carelessness, and frequently destroyed that they may not fall into the hands of the enemy. These circumstances operated to a greater extent than usual, in proportion as the number of British soldiers and sailors, and the cost at which each man was maintained, were beyond all former example. The supply of provisions from other countries

was at the same time restricted, both by the idle-
ness and waste attendant on political convulsions,
and still more directly by the circumstance of
those countries from which in times of scarcity
we are accustomed to draw our corn, being frequently in alliance with, or in the military possession of, our enemy. For several years, also,
our armies acting in the peninsula, which
even during peace does not support its own inhabitants, depended entirely for subsistence, and
in a great measure even for forage, on the crops
raised or imported into Britain. To all this it
may be added, that from unfavourable seasons,
two uncommon scarcities occurred in 1796 and
1800, during which corn rose to an almost unexampled price.

The extraordinary demand for agricultural
produce arising from those causes, joined to the
depreciation of our currency to be afterwards
noticed, enriched the farmers during their
leases, and occasioned a remarkable advance
both of the rent and value of land. Agricul-

tural speculations seemed to enrich every one who engaged in them ; capital, as might be expected, rushed to this employment ; a competition arose for labour, by which the wages of farm servants were rapidly advanced; and the general style of cultivation was improved, and large tracks of land were rendered fit for tillage, at an expense which, in other circumstances, would have been altogether ruinous.

In ordinary cases, the encouragement which the consequent expenditure of farmers and landholders held out to arts and commerce, would have been in a great degree counteracted by the loss of foreign markets, and the decay of the carrying trade. The destruction of capital by the war-expenditure, and the drawing off so large a proportion of it to agriculture, would have diminished the manufacturing and trading stock, and raised the rate of profit; the demand for country labour would have raised every description of wages; and the consequent high prices of our goods would have checked their consumption both at home and abroad.

In this respect Britain stood in a situation entirely new. Partly by the undisputed sovereignty of the sea, which she obtained early in the war, and exercised, perhaps with policy, certainly without regard to justice; partly by the revolutions in Europe, which, whatever may be their ultimate effects, were, at their commencement, destructive of manufacturing industry; partly by the astonishing exertions of the French to recruit their armies at home, and partly, too, by their unparalleled victories, which enabled them, without much consideration for the welfare of their subjects and allies, forcibly to recruit them in the conquered countries: by these circumstances we were enabled, on the one hand, to obstruct the entry of the materials of manufacture into the rest of Europe, while, on the other hand, the manufacturing capital, and the manufacturing population of the continent, were nearly annihilated. Thus

Britain, during the course of the war, acquired and maintained a kind of monopoly of
the commerce of the world; and, accordingly, however high agricultural profits and labour
were raised, those of trade accompanied, if they
did not outstrip, them.

In such a state of prosperity, the annual accumulation of wealth by individual economy
might be expected to compensate, in a great
degree, probably entirely, the unproductive expenditure, however wasteful, of the state. But
it was not enough that the national capital
should be preserved; for unless it had been
very greatly increased, there must soon have
been a limit to the extension of our trade.
This necessary increase of capital was derived
from many sources. Commotions in various
parts of Europe induced foreign capitalists to
remit to this country, as a place of safety, those
funds which they thought endangered at home:
the substitution of paper for a metallic currency
restored to productive purposes a considerable ca-

pital, which had formerly been a mere implement
of exchange: the eager demand for our commodities abroad, and their rapid sale, enabled our manufacturers to recover the possession of their capitals in a shorter period than usual, and consequently, with the same stock, to put in motion a
much greater quantity of industry: and partly
from want of confidence in foreign merchants,
but chiefly from the increased difference between
cash and credit prices consequent on high profits, our commodities were very generally sold
to foreign countries for ready money; so that
the large British capital that, through protracted credits, used to remain abroad, was now called home, and rendered available for British production.

Even the demand for our goods, unexampled
as it was, and the possession of capital sufficient
for their manufacture, must have failed in producing their full effects on national wealth, had
there been no means of increasing our population except by the children of marriages con-

tracted in consequence of the new demand for labour. No immigration having taken place, wages would have risen so high as to check consumption both at home and abroad. But here the genius of our Wedgewoods, our Arkwrights, and our Watts, came powerfully to the aid of national prosperity. The inventions of these and many other eminent men, and the intelligence of our ordinary workmen stimulated by the high rewards held out to ingenuity, abundantly supplied our wants. Old inventions were improved, new machines were constructed, uncommon exertions were called forth by the almost universal establishment of task work, and the ordinary limits of human power seemed for a time to be effaced.

But this prosperity could not last, far less could it keep pace with the lavish expenditure of the war; and before the conclusion of peace, there were abundant symptoms of its having reached its summit, and even of its having begun to decline.

The demand for agricultural produce was supported by the increase of our population, the augmentation of our military force, the employment of a large army in the peninsula, and the difficulties thrown in the way of importing grain ; yet so much had been done in bringing in new lands, and ameliorating the old, that rents seemed to have reached their highest point, and to be more likely to retrograde than to advance. The expenditure of the proprietors, however, which had risen with their rentals, could not easily be again reduced, and the increasing taxes, particularly the property tax, now pressed heavily on a stationary income. Many, in place of retrenchment, had recourse to the ruinous expedient of borrowing on extravagant terms ; and, notwithstanding the great and important addition that had been made to the rent-roll of the country, pecuniary difficulties, long before the termination of the war, threatened ruin to small proprietors, and extreme embarrassment even to those possessed of princely estates.

The high profits of trade were still less of a permanent nature. The continental nations, being rapidly impoverished both by the ravages and expenses of the war, became less able, from year to year, to purchase our goods, loaded as they were by increased wages, profits, and taxes in this country, and by enormous risks and charges of transportation. What foreigners could no longer afford, they were obliged to dispense with; and, before the close of the war, our extensive manufacturing establishments had frequently to complain of glutted markets. Our enemies became sensible that, in our monopoly of trade we found our most ample resources; and the Milan Decrees, originating partly in this conviction, and partly, too, in indignation at the unsparing exercise of our naval preponderance, aimed a deadly blow at our prosperity. Such, however, was our superiority in manufacture, and so great the disinclination of our foreign customers to deny themselves luxuries to which they had long been accustomed, that those decrces would have had little other effect than to raise in some measure the price of the goods we furnished, and in so far to discourage their consumption, had we not, with an impolicy rarely paralleled, given them fatal efficacy, by our retaliatory Orders in Council.

These orders, disapproved of from the first by every one acquainted with the nature of our trade, were tardily recalled, in consequence of the almost universal distress which they brought on our artizans, manufacturers, and merchants; but not till this distress, by discovering our vulnerable part, had encouraged Napoleon to continue and extend his restrictive system; not till the total inability to procure our commodities had taught the nations of the continent that the use of some of them might be dispensed with, and that tolerable substitutes for others might be found at home.

A similar impolicy, urged on by the cupidity

of our ship-owners, who seemed to think it a grievous injury that any vessels but their own should presume to navigate the ocean, and perhaps embittered by an old and illiberal grudge, engaged us first in disputes, and afterwards in hostilities, with the only nation except our own that had prospered by the war. In America we saw only a rival, when we might have seen our best and steadiest customer: her intercourse with Europe we viewed as an interference with our commercial monopoly, when we ought to have been sensible that it afforded us the best and almost only means of eluding those artificial barriers that were raised up against our trade. Severe punishment awaited our short-sighted rapacity. Our merchants found it necessary to descend from the high character which they had always maintained, and to carry on their commerce through the medium of smugglers, traffickers in forged documents, and suborners of perjury. But their contrivances, however various and artful, were frequently detected, and on several occasions, the project of excluding us from Europe seemed more than an empty threat.

Trade now became a lottery. At one time our warehouses, both at home and abroad, were filled with goods for which no market could be found; our artizans, thrown idle, were supported by charity; our manufacturers and merchants became embarrassed or bankrupt. At another time, some partial relaxation of the continental system required for the convenience of our enemy, a new and successful fraud by which the vigilance of revenue officers was for a moment eluded, or a desire for our goods so vehement that it could not safely be opposed, relieved our overflowing warehouses, gave new activity to our manufactures, raised some merchants to sudden opulence, and sunk in total ruin those whose cargoes arrived a few weeks later to glutted markets.

Wearied with such vicissitudes, and hoping for a more steady, if not a more lucrative or extended, trade, the nation hailed with general acclamation the approach of peace. But peace did not, as she was wont, bring prosperity in her train.

The demand for agricultural produce declined of course, and farmers, who had taken their lands at extravagant rents, were involved in difficulties, which the variations in the currency, to be afterwards noticed, converted into ruin. There was no longer any temptation to improve new lands, or encouragement to follow out the best system of culture in the old. It became the object of every farmer to save expense, as the most probable means of avoiding loss; in consequence of which, farm servants were soon obliged to submit to a reduction of wages, and at no distant time numbers of them were deprived of work.

As tenants became bankrupt, or their leases expired, there was regularly a reduction of rent. Yet so great had been the increase of population and the amelioration of the land, that there can be no doubt of the aggregate rental of the kingdom, after all these reductions, being still much higher than at the commencement of the war; and, allowance being made for the change in the currency, by which the new rents are in reality twenty-five, or perhaps thirty, per cent. nearer to the old than their nominal amounts, it is most probable that the repeal of the property tax left those landholders who are free from debt, as opulent as they had been at any period of the war*. Their means of expenditure, though many suffered from the failure of their tenants, were not otherwise reduced by the peace; but all other sources of demand for our manufactures experienced a rapid decline.

---

* This opinion, it will be seen, proceeds on the assumption that the fall of rents from the decrease of the demand for produce, apart from that greater nominal fall occasioned by the restoration of the currency to its former value, has not exceeded 10 per cent.—the rate of the property tax. Whether this assumption be correct, I have no means of ascertaining.

It must be observed, however, that the addition to the income of landholders, by the repeal of the property tax, made no addition to the demand for our goods, as great a proportion at least of public revenue, as of that enjoyed by landholders, being usually expended on home productions. Even the demand therefore created by the expenditure of landed proprietors, when this circumstance is taken into view, might probably suffer some decrease, though small in comparison with what necessarily followed the decline of profits and of wages.

Extensive works, adapted to the supply of our own army and navy, and of those both of our allies and our enemies, were rendered useless and abandoned, the capital sunk in them being lost, and the workmen discharged, to add to the overstock of hands already beginning to be felt in other employments. In proportion to the extent of our warlike exertions, and to the monopoly we had enjoyed of supplying all the belligerents with clothing, accoutrements, and warlike stores, must have been the revulsion occasioned by the instantaneous annihilation of so great and so lucrative a trade.

Our manufactures being now freed from the charges, risks, and obstructions occasioned by the war, some compensation might have been expected, as in former times, by the opening up of new markets, and the extension of the old. But in this our merchants were disappointed. The nations of the continent were too much impoverished to be able to purchase the usual quantity of our manufactures, even at reduced rates; and in many situations, the people had been so long deprived of them, that their habits were broken, and they had learned to be content with various substitutions. It being again in their power to procure the raw material for themselves, the cheapness of labour, occasioned by the reduction of their armies, and by the decay of their wealth, induced many of them to attempt home manufactures. In spite of this cheapness, however, they found themselves undersold in their own countries, by British traders now pushing off their goods in every market at prices far below the cost; and the ruin which thus threatened their infant establishments, aided by the dislike of Britain which had sprung from the imperious exercise of her naval power, inclined the people to demand, and their governments to enact, restrictive or prohibitory laws against the introduction of British goods.

What then became the condition of this country? With establishments adapted to the supply of the world, we were in a great measure thrown back on our own consumption; and this at a time when that consumption also was diminished by the low returns of mercantile and farming capital, and by a great reduction of the rate of wages. Two consequences followed, which some systems represent as necessarily of very short duration, but which our experience has proved to be evils of no ordinary magnitude. There was an excess of capital, which for years has been unable to find any advantageous employment; and the profits of stock, in place of rising, as we are told they must do, on the decline of wages, have sunk along with them, and fully to as great an extent.

In this state of things, some of the works erected for the supply both of home and foreign demand have been partially or entirely stopped, and others have been carried on, not because they yield any thing that can be considered as rent, but from unwillingness to abandon such costly establishments, and in the hopes of better times. Circulating capital, though not thus annihilated, has been so very unproductive, that more loss than profit, it is generally believed, has resulted from commercial transactions. The wealth of the nation must consequently have declined, in as far as the expenditure of the mercantile classes has exceeded the interest of their capitals; while the money transmitted to this country, during the war, has been recalled, and part of

our own capital has gone abroad directly as
loans, and probably much more of it indirectly in credits, to other countries, where, from
the impoverishment occasioned by the war, and
the new branches of employment opened up by
the peace, it is more in request.

Of all the evils resulting from the war and
its termination, by far the most distressing has
been the want of employment for the people.
So great was the demand for labour, and so
high its wages, that the population of Britain
advanced with unusual rapidity; and this encouragement having lasted, with occasional fluctuations, for above twenty years, the number of
our people had become nearly sufficient to supply
even this extraordinary demand. The stagnation
of every branch of industry that followed the conclusion of peace, aggravated by the necessary
reduction of our army and navy, and by the
discharge of workmen from our arsenals and
dock-yards, as well as from those extensive
manufactures that had been established for the

equipment of all the belligerent armies, soon reduced wages to so low a rate, that all our workmen were obliged to submit to the severest privations, and many, being unable to find employment even at reduced wages, were forced to subsist on public alms. The distress, general as it was over all the country, and in every branch of industry, was particularly severe in those manufacturing districts where goods were prepared for the consumption of the lower orders no longer able to purchase them, or for exportation to those parts of Europe impoverished by the war, or shut against us by the jealousy of trade.

Such is a rapid and imperfect sketch of the evils that have accompanied the transition from a long and expensive war, to a state of peace; or rather, which have resulted from the singular excitement of this country, and the impoverishment of the Continent, during long protracted hostilities. To remedy them at once by any legislative measure, would be a hopeless at-

tempt. But they may be expected gradually
to disappear as Europe recovers from her losses,
and, finding beneficial employment for her capital in agriculture, or such arts as her states are
peculiarly fitted to cultivate, she becomes willing again to receive from us those articles which
we can furnish on the cheapest terms*.

To promote this desirable change, perhaps all
that we can do is to mitigate, if we cannot remove, the restrictions of our commercial code; to
soften by such means that jealousy which represents us, not altogether unjustly, as grasping at
a monopoly of the commerce of the world; and
to show, by a great practical example, that our
prosperity has not arisen, as is believed by some
persons at home, and many abroad, from our illiberal policy, but has been repressed and

---

* Even at this time [February 1821] a considerable improvement seems to have taken place in almost all the manufacturing districts. The people are now employed; and though
their wages are still low, they are able, from the cheapness of
provisions, to maintain their families.

shackled by every departure from perfect free-dom of trade. Difficulties of no ordinary mag-nitude undoubtedly oppose any rash and sweep-ing repeal of a system of restrictions so closely interwoven with the frame of our commercial and manufacturing establishments*. But if we

---

* While fully aware of the difficulty of altering our navi-gation laws, not on account of any advantage that is, or ever has been, derived from them, either to our commerce or our navy, but solely on account of the claim which our ship-owners may have to privileges of long standing, I cannot approve of the excessive timidity that seems to pervade the late report [July 1820] of a committee on this subject to the House of Commons. What our merchants require, is to be allowed to carry on their trade in the cheapest manner; what foreign na-tions insist upon is, that their ships shall have the same free admission into our ports, that ours have into theirs. What the committee seems to propose, is, to alter our navigation laws, whenever it is certain that by so doing one British ship the less, or one foreign ship the more, shall not be employed; that is, whenever it is of no consequence whatever, whether the restriction be repealed or maintained. Perhaps this mode of reasoning may have been adopted by the committee, to dis-arm opposition from the great body of ship-owners; but I should think it more manly to say at once, that though every attention will be paid to their claims arising from the present laws of the land, they can no longer be permitted to raise taxes

are really desirous of returning to a more liberal policy, improvements may be adopted, which will promote our intercourse with other countries, conciliate their favour, or at least soften their prejudices; and, by our actions, at length proclaim our adherence to that great fundamental maxim of Political Economy, which teaches that our prosperity must be derived from the wealth, not the poverty, of surrounding nations.

SECTION II.

EFFECTS OF THE ALTERATIONS IN OUR CURRENCY.

It is now unnecessary to prove that, subsequently to the Bank Restriction Act, our currency

on their fellow citizens for their own benefit, or to furnish foreign states with unanswerable arguments for shackling our commerce.

fell into a state of great depreciation ; this being a fact on which even the factious vote of the House of Commons in 1811 cannot throw the slightest doubt. It is not, however, so certain that the fall of the pound sterling, from its former value in comparison of commodities, was accurately measured, either by the price of gold, or the state of the foreign exchanges. It is possible that the value of gold might have risen in Europe, and that consequently our currency might not have fallen from its former value to the degree intimated by its inferiority to the advanced price of the precious metals either at home or abroad. In other words, the depreciation might not be absolute compared to the value of commodities, but relative compared to the new value of gold and silver, and therefore to the currencies of those countries which continued to use gold and silver as their ordinary medium of purchase and sale.

In how far this hypothesis (for in the absence of any fixed standard of value, it could only be a hypothesis) was correct, it is almost impossible to determine. On the one hand, the demand for gold, for the purposes of so extended a warfare, was likely to occasion some rise in its value; the precious metals, like every thing else, depending for their value on use and demand. On the other hand, recourse was so generally had to paper currency, both in Europe and America, that the gold and silver which were displaced from circulation, must have gone far in supplying the increased demand occasioned by the war.

According as the one or the other of these circumstances preponderated, supposing the produce of the mines to have remained unaltered, the absolute must have been either less or more than the relative depreciation of our currency. Considering the large sums supplied for the use of the armies, and of those countries that retained a metallic currency, by the very general substitution of paper, the probability would rather seem to be, that the depreciation in this country was greater than it appeared; and this inference is strengthened by the general rise which took place in the price of goods, even when they were paid for in gold—a rise which, if universal, would be equivalent to a decline in the value of that metal.

However this may be, no reasonable doubt can be entertained of the currency of Britain, in the progress of the war, having been depreciated to a great degree, both absolutely and relatively; and of the enhancement of the prices of all labour and goods at home, having been the consequence of the one, while the high price of gold, and unfavourable foreign exchanges, were undeniable proofs of the other.

By this depreciation, annuitants, and others possessing fixed incomes in sterling money, were materially injured; the real nature of every contract for a term of years was altered, to the gain of the one party and the loss of the other; public and private creditors were defrauded of part of their rights; but the agriculture, manufactures, and commerce of the country, were for a time encouraged.

During current leases, the farmer, without any rise on his rent, had all the advantage of the high price of corn consequent on the depreciation of money, and was thus both induced and enabled to improve his farm at the expense of his landlord. When leases expired, however, rents regularly advanced; so that before the termination of the war, farming profit, on lands recently let, had been reduced to a moderate rate, and the landlord found a compensation for the temporary loss to which he had at first been subjected, in a large addition to his ordinary rental. In so far as this addition was merely equivalent to the depreciation of currency, it was nominal, making him no richer than before. But the encouragement that had been given to agriculture, had induced his tenants to lay out part of their unusual gains in the amelioration of the land; and the rise of rent, in as far as it had its origin in superior cultivation and increased production, was a permanent benefit to the landholder and the country.

At the same time, the gradual fall in the value of money, produced a corresponding rise in the price of all kinds of goods. The manufacturer, while working up the raw material; the merchant, between the time of his importation and his sales; the retailer upon the stock of goods in his shop; each of them found himself richer from week to week, without being aware that this influx of wealth was chiefly nominal. After selling one assortment to great apparent advantage, the merchant must have found, that it required nearly the usual proportion of the proceeds to furnish himself with a new supply; but by farther depreciation of money, this new stock also seemed to yield an ample return, and the annual balance of his books exhibited the appearance of rapid increase in the pounds sterling, according to which he was accustomed to estimate his wealth. Every speculation seemed to be profitable, whether proceeding on extensive information, or on mere disregard of risk; and the spirit of mercantile gambling, arising from other circumstances that have been stated, was fostered by this semblance of success. Each person became anxious to secure the greatest possible share of the prizes in this immense lottery; and bankers, desirous of extending their circulation to the utmost, and little afraid of danger while all their customers seemed prosperous, supplied in profusion the means of extensive speculation.

All this factitious activity took place too at a time when, from other causes already noticed, there was a great and increasing demand for our goods, and while the substitution of paper for a metallic currency was turning wealth of no small amount, which had formerly been unproductive, into real and efficient mercantile capital*.

* The estimates that have been formed of the quantity of gold required for a metallic currency in Britain are so much at

From all these circumstances combined, there was a rise in the wages of labour, not only commensurate to the depreciation of the currency and the advance in the price of necessaries, but also (from the difficulty of procuring the number of workmen requisite to keep pace with the demand for goods), sufficient, except in a few seasons of sterility or of glutted markets, to spread an uncommon degree of comfort among the people.

But when our currency began to rise towards its former value, after the conclusion of the peace, the picture was sadly reversed.

Some classes of the people, indeed, derived great and positive advantages from the change. Those annuitants, whose incomes had been reduced by the depreciation, were restored to their former situation in life, and others, who had pur-

---

variance with each other, and formed on such unsatisfactory data, that it is useless to refer to any of them.

chased or succeeded to annuities during the war, were enriched.   All creditors also, whether public or private, received a great accession to their wealth at the expense of their debtors. The interest, to which they were entitled by their contracts, enabled them to live more comfortably, as the value of the pound sterling in the purchase of goods advanced, and they drew back their capital, when they had occasion for it, in a currency which had been improved in some cases 20, and in others 40 per cent.

But the restoration of the currency, by which those classes were enriched, seemed to have a very opposite effect on the situation of all other members of the community.

Farmers who had taken leases at extravagant money rents, were ruined by that fall of prices which arose partly from the diminished demand, and partly also from improvement of the currency, and, being unable to continue any expensive system of culture, tried in vain to save themselves by discharging their labourers, and underworking their lands. When the landlord gave a deduction of rent corresponding to the change that was taking place in the value of money, he in reality received all that had been stipulated, his income, though nominally reduced, being able to purchase as many commodities as before; and he enabled his farmer to struggle, with some prospect of success, against the other difficulties of his situation. When the terms of the lease were enforced, the tenant, after having materially injured the land, became bankrupt, and the farm was let anew, at a rent reduced, not only by the rise of the currency, but also by the general situation of the country, and the deterioration of the farm itself.

Few of the landholders, unfortunately for themselves and for the country, have taken a sufficiently enlarged and liberal view of the contracts into which their tenants had entered, while the currency was depreciated. It is scarcely to be expected, indeed, that he who has a legal right to L.500 a year, should voluntarily restrict it to L.370, or even to L.410; yet the one would be the fair and just rent, if the farm was let in 1813, when the price of gold was L.5. 6s. per oz.; and the other if the lease commenced in 1810, when it was L.4. 15s. It is not surprising that, in such circumstances, many proprietors should endeavour to maintain their rents at their former nominal rates, and that others should consider a partial and inadequate reduction, as an action of uncommon generosity. But it is perfectly obvious that this ineffectual struggle to maintain the nominal rent, after the value of the currency has undergone so material a change, is the main cause of that agricultural distress, of which the country gentlemen of England so loudly complain. The remedy is in their own hands; and if they will not apply it, it is in vain for them to appoint committees, or to attempt to accomplish that by legislation, which in its own nature is unattainable.

The price of corn, it is true, is low, but not so very low as it appears to be, when contrasted with the prices to which, partly in consequence of the depreciation of the currency, it had been raised. Sixty shillings a quarter at present, are equal to seventy-three in 1810, and to eighty-three in 1813 ; and when it is considered that butcher meat is at a higher price than before the commencement of the war, and that the average price of wheat for several years previous to 1793, was about fifty-eight shillings, there may be some reason to doubt whether farm-produce in general is very greatly depressed below what is likely to be its ordinary value during peace.

By the mere return of the currency to its pristine value, the landholders, whether they reduced their rents voluntarily, or after ruining their tenants, suffered nothing. If they got fewer pounds sterling, each pound was of greater value in the purchase of goods ; and they retained permanently all that addition to their rental which resulted from the farmers having laid out a large capital in adding to the productive qualities of the land *.

---

* Those landholders who, during the war, had borrowed money, whether for their ordinary expenses, or the improvement of their estates, have undoubtedly suffered severely by the change from a depreciated currency. In common with all other debtors, they are now forced to pay the same nominal interest, from nominally reduced incomes; and when they wish to discharge the principal of the debt, they must do it in a currency one-fourth, or perhaps one-third, more valuable than that in which the obligation was contracted.

Had they understood the consequences of the restoration of the currency, many would have preferred the adoption of Lord Lauderdale's proposal of fixing the value of the pound sterling at the low rate to which it had fallen—a measure by which both the landholders and the state would have been protected from increased burdens for the benefit of their creditors*. Whether equal injustice, though to other classes, would have resulted from this expedient, will depend on the number of existing contracts entered into before 1808, compared with those of a later date. Perhaps this was a case in which a half measure was the most desirable; and I am rather inclined to think that it would have been better to have fixed the mint price of gold at L. 4. 5s. or L.4. 10s. sterling, than to have adopted either the old mint price, or that

* See Farther Considerations on the State of the Currency, by the Earl of Lauderdale—a tract which deserved much more serious consideration from the Legislature than it seems to have received.

But it was otherwise with the mercantile classes. The goods in their possession fell in price from day to day, as the value of the currency improved; and on every transaction, particularly on those in which the investment was of considerable duration, there appeared to be loss in place of profit. Every manufacturer, therefore, discharged his workmen, or limited their employment; every merchant contracted his importations, which occasioned a corresponding diminution of our exports; and every retailer reduced his stock as low as he could venture to do without displeasing his customers, and permanently losing his trade.

While matters were in this state, bankers were forced to withdraw part of the accommodation on which the merchants had been led to rely. On the one hand, the risk of discounting bills

---

very high price to which gold, for several years, had been raised.

was greatly increased, by the unsaleableness of goods, and the heavy loss occurring from forced sales; and on the other hand, the apprehension of a speedy return to a metallic currency, made it indispensable that bankers should contract their circulation, and have their capitals at command. A very general state of embarrassment was the result, and bankruptcies to an unexampled extent soon completed the distress.

The unsteadiness of the Bank of England added greatly to the disorder. After the market price of gold had fallen nearly to that of the mint*, and every disadvantage attending the return to an undepreciated currency had been already incurred, for reasons which could not have been conjectured, had not the examination of the bank directors by the committee of the House of Commons in 1819 disclosed

---

* From July 1816 to July 1817.

the most surprising ignorance of the plainest truths of Political Economy*, they allowed the price of gold again to advance.   The consequences of this new depreciation of the currency were a new degree of activity in almost every branch of trade and manufacture, and a fleeting semblance of commercial prosperity, speedily followed by numerous bankruptcies and redoubled distress.

Thus it appears, that the state of the currency powerfully aided those other circumstances, by the operation of which the return of peace became a season of adversity.   Its effects, however, in this view, were only temporary ; and as the market price of gold has now for more than a year and a half been the same with the mint price, our currency must have risen to its

---

* Mr Haldimand's evidence forms a striking and honourable exception.

proper level, and most of the evils of the transition are probably past.

But there is one consequence of the depreciation during the war, which unhappily is of a permanent nature.

While the value of our money was at the lowest, our war expenses were unfortunately at the highest. Had the supplies been raised within the year, this would have been of little importance; for if a greater number of pounds sterling had been expended, each pound was of inferior value. But at that period, loans to an immense amount were contracted, and taxes were imposed to pay the interest, and gradually to refund the capital of those loans. The sum to be paid to the public creditor was fixed when the value of money was low, and the same nominal sum must still be levied from the nation, though that value has greatly advanced. Nor was any compensation got, in the terms of the loans, for this heavy and permanent burden that was unnecessarily brought on the nation.   The loan contractors, having no intention of holding their stock till the peace, made their offers only according to the price which they expected in a few months to realise by sale ; and so uncertain was the period when the course of depreciation might be stopt, so much more uncertain that at which, if ever, our currency should be again raised to its former value, that this distant, and, as many thought, improbable, contingency, could not in the slightest degree affect the market price of the funds. The taxes therefore imposed during the greatest depreciation, are now one-fourth, some of them one-third, higher than they were at the time, or than they would have been had our currency been maintained on a par with its nominal value.

If, then, we shall afterwards find reason to at-tribute the distresses of the people to the amount of the taxes levied from the nation, it must be obvious that no inconsiderable part of this evil is to be traced to the Bank Restriction Act, and the depreciation of currency which ensued*.

SECTION III.

EFFECTS OF THE WAR-EXPENDITURE.

The conversion of capital into unproductive expenditure during war, and the consequent impoverishment of the belligerent nations, have

---

* The following Table, without pretending to accuracy, will give some idea of the amount of taxes unnecessarily imposed on England, during twelve years of the late war. The first column contains the charge for interest and management of all the loans and fundings of Exchequer Bills, in each year; and is taken from Dr Hamilton's Inquiry into the National Debt, Part ii. chap. 1. sect. 2. The second and third columns are chiefly taken from Lord Lauderdale's Farther Considerations on the State of the Currency, third column

so generally resulted from protracted hostilities, that it is natural to ascribe the depressed state of industry and commerce in this country, in part at least, to this cause.

---

of Appendix XI. and third column of Appendix I. The fourth column is calculated from the first and third.

		Amount of Taxes on account of Loans. &c.	Average price of Gold.		Depreciation of the currency per pound sterling.		Extra permanent Taxes arising from the depreciation.
1804	Loan..........	L.552,158	L.4	0	0s.	6½d.	L.14,954
1805	Do.	1,043,696	4	0	0s.	6½d.	28,267
1806	Do.	906,559	4	0	0s.	6½d.	24,552
1807	Do.	583,307	4	0	0s.	6½d.	15,798
1808	Do. and Exchequer Bills........	640,440	4	9	2s.	10¼d.	91,396
1809	Do. and do..	928,116	4	11	3s.	4½d.	156,619
1810	Do. and do..	772,690	4	15	4s.	4¾d.	169,828
1811	Do. and do..	941,196	5	1	5s.	11¼d.	279,417
1812	Do. and do..	1,203,422	5	8	7s.	8¾d.	465,072
1813	Two Budgets and Exchequer Bills........	3,259,052	5	6	7s.	2¾d.	1,178,011
1814	Loan..........	859,242 *	4	16	4s.	7¾d.	199,594
1815	Do. and Exchequer Bills........	2,599,085 *	4	12	3s.	7½d.	471,084
		L. 14,288,963					L.3,094,592

* Appendix, No. XIV. to Report of the House of Commons 6th May 1819.

In whatever manner war-supplies are levied, they usually, nearly to their whole amount, reduce the capital of the country. If they be

---

When it is considered that this Table goes back only to 1804, although large loans were contracted for in each of the four preceding years, with a currency somewhat depreciated, there can be no doubt that, even without farther retrenchment of any kind, not only would the taxes imposed in 1819 have been unnecessary, but, independently of them, there would have been a larger sinking fund than at present, had not the currency been depreciated at the time that the debt was contracted.

Previously to Mr Pitt's death in 1806, the depreciation of the currency was to be reprobated rather for the danger of the example, than the extent of the evil. But while Mr Percival was Chancellor of Exchequer, this cautious system was neglected, and, after the memorable vote of the House of Commons, on the Bullion question, in 1811, openly abandoned. Upon Mr Percival's assassination in 1812, Mr Vansittart (as it would appear, on account of the ignorance or compliance which he had displayed on the Bullion question) was set at the head of the Finances, and the result was such as might have been anticipated. When Mr Pitt thought himself forced by circumstances into a path which he could not approve, he advanced with cautious and timid steps: his successors, though professing to model all their opinions and actions upon his, being profoundly ignorant of the first principles of Political Economy, proceeded in their destructive career with gigantic strides.

raised within the year, each contributor will be obliged to withdraw his portion of the supplies from his own trade, or to borrow it from his friends, or to demand it from those to whom it was lent, and by whom it was productively em-

---

No doubt, the depreciation must be attributed, in the first instance, to the Bank of England; but Ministers could, at any time, have checked the evil; and when we cast our eyes on the following Tables, extracted from Appendix III. to the Report of the Secret Committee of the House of Commons, 6th .May 1819, we shall not be much at a loss to discover the reasons of Government having acquiesced, without remonstrance, in the excess of paper issued by the Bank, and the consequent depreciation of the currency.

It may be proper to premise, that I have taken a mean between the advances of the Bank to Government, on the 26th February and 26th August of each year.

TABLE, showing the advances of the Bank to Government, immediately before and after the Bank Restriction.

Year.	Amount.	
1794	L. 9,777,336	
1795	13,289,078	
1796	11,585,926	Bank Restriction Act in February 1797.
1797	8,663,498	
1798	9,626,395	

ployed. If, on the other hand, the war expenses are defrayed by a public loan, the subscribers to the loan must, in the same manner, recal their funds from their former productive employments, and lend them to the state for the purpose of unproductive expenditure. In either way, the capital of the nation is equally reduced.

Some additional economy is no doubt encouraged, by the disinclination felt by many to that decay of their fortunes, which is either made quite apparent by the visit of the tax-gatherer to collect the war supplies, or suggested, though

---

TABLE, showing the advances of the Bank to Government in each year, from 1805 to 1814 inclusive.

Year.	Amount.	
1805	L.14,479,039	
1806	14,554,339	Mr Pitt died.
1807	13,714,439	
1808	15,021,239	
1809	15,703,739	
1810	16,355,789	
1811	20,382,339	Mr Vansittart's Resolutions on Bullion question.
1812	22,254,689	Mr Percival assassinated.
1813	25,812,639	
1814	30,149,289	

neither quite so directly, nor to the same extent, by the rise of the articles of consumption on which taxes are imposed to pay the interest of the annual loans. But if this additional economy be sufficient, in the one case, to cover the profit that is lost by the change of part of each man's wealth from productive capital to public contribution, or, in the other case, to keep the family expenditure, notwithstanding the new taxes, nearly about its former amount, this is all that can be expected; the whole of the contribution, or the whole of the loan, being a deduction from the previously existing wealth of the nation*. Every year of a war, in ordinary circumstances, must thus diminish the fund destined to the employment of labour, to its own reproduction, and to the creation of profit; and for such diminution of capital, national impoverishment may be considered as a synonimous term.

---

* These views are much more fully illustrated in Elements of Political Science, Book. III, Part. iii. chap. 1.

It is impossible to deny that this is the usual, almost the constant, effect of war on national wealth; and although I have no very direct information on the subject, I have little doubt that this effect has been severely felt in the greater part of the continent of Europe. But that Britain has escaped, in this particular, the ordinary consequence of war must be obvious to any one who looks round to the high cultivation of the land, the growth of the towns, the multiplication of canals, the rise of manufacturing establishments, and the general improvement in the houses, furniture, and style of living of the middle ranks of society.

The present state of mercantile affairs leads to the same conclusion. The very low rate of mercantile profit is a sufficient proof, that capital is not deficient, but redundant. Every person entitled to credit, it is well known, can easily procure sufficient funds for his ordinary trade, or even for extensive occasional speculations; and no sooner is any adventure believed to yield profit, than there is a rush of capital towards it, by which, in a very short time, the market is overstocked.

The causes of this anomalous condition of Britain, after a long war and most wasteful expenditure, I have already endeavoured to trace; and if I be not extremely incorrect, both in facts and reasoning, it is impossible to contend that any part of our present difficulties has its origin in national impoverishment.

But the Earl of Lauderdale, in an ingenious protest entered on the journals of the House of Lords*, has given a new view of the manner, in which he is of opinion that the war-expenditure has brought on our present commercial languor.

As the enormous expenditure of the war could not be defrayed by the parsimony of indi-

----

* 17th December 1819.

viduals, each year must have converted what was formerly private capital, into public revenue to be immediately consumed. By this excess of annual consumption, he conceives that a new demand, nearly to the extent of the war-expenditure, was added to that which exists during peace; and that the consequences of this unusual demand were high profits, and the multiplication of manufacturing and commercial establishments all over the country. The peace at once put an end to an enormous expenditure of the national capital, and with it to a prodigious demand for the produce of our industry, arising from that expenditure; and to the limitation of the demand for goods to what could be purchased by the annual income of individuals, while we had been accustomed, for a number of years, likewise to consume a considerable portion of our own capital, and to supply the demand created by a similar consumption of the capital of the other belligerent powers, his Lordship ascribes much the greatest part of the stagnation which ensued.

While I fully admit that the diminution of demand for our goods has been the main cause of almost all the distress we have suffered, I cannot adopt the reasonings by which Lord Lauderdale accounts for that reduction of demand, by the termination of our own war-expenditure.

I have already endeavoured to show, in Chapter III., that circulating capital is annually consumed as regularly as income, though by a different set of people; capital by hired workmen, the produce of whose labour restores it, with a profit, to its proprietor; income by the proprietor himself, without any kind of reproduction, for his own gratification. No new demand therefore arises from changing capital into income, but merely an alteration of the persons by whom it is consumed, together with this material difference, that there is no longer any new production in consequence of that consumption.

According to the class of individuals by

whom the capital or income is annually consumed, there may indeed be considerable difference in the degree in which the same expenditure will encourage home or foreign industry.
In general, a much greater number of the articles used by the lower orders are of home
growth and manufacture, than of those required
by the rich; and therefore the annual consumption of capital by workmen affords more encouragement to domestic industry, than that of an
equal amount of the revenues of the opulent.
But in this respect, war-expenses very much resemble the expenses of the lower orders, being
laid out in great measure in pay to soldiers, and
in provisions, clothing, accoutrements, ammuni-
tion, and naval stores, for the most part produced at home. The change of capital to war-
expenditure may not in this view be unfavourable to domestic industry; but as it can scarcely
give it any new encouragement, the total demand for goods, even in the first year of hostilities, will not be increased, though the particu-

lar description of goods brought into demand will be considerably varied.

In every successive year, the demand, in place of increasing in consequence of the war-expenditure, will regularly decline. What was formerly capital, being now consumed by the state without reproduction, ceases to exist. The consumption of the second year must therefore be less than that of the first, by the amount both of the capital thus extinguished, and of the profit which it used to produce. The third year's consumption will be still decreased as the capital and profits are farther diminished; and thus, were we to confine our view to this one circumstance, we should arrive at a conclusion very opposite to that of Lord Lauderdale; for the war-expenditure, in place of swelling the annual consumption and demand, must have annually contracted them in a remarkable degree.

The return of peace, though it cannot restore

the capital already squandered, puts an immediate stop to the progress of national impoverishment, and to that limitation of demand for goods, which is its necessary consequence. In the first year of peace, the amount of the whole capital and income of the nation is the same as in the last year of the preceding war; and therefore, though the description of goods in demand will be extremely different, the total quantity of goods required, by the expenditure of the capital and income of the nation together, will be the same. Private parsimony will then begin to repair the waste occasioned by the war; and exactly as it proceeds in restoring the capital that had been squandered, the whole annual revenue of the society, and the demand for goods occasioned by the annual consumption of that revenue, will regularly increase.

Such has probably been the general progress of the continental states, rapidly impoverished during the war, and now beginning to repair their losses under the happy re-establishment of

peace. It is indeed mainly to the prosperity
and gradual enrichment of other nations, that
we may look with confidence for a revival of our
trade ; and it may perhaps be ultimately fortunate for us, that we have been placed in circumstances, in which even the most prejudiced
must be sensible that the welfare of Britain is
entirely dependent on that of the rest of Europe.
But both during the war, and since the peace,
Britain has found herself in a situation of which
there are few examples. Her wealth, increased
rather than diminished in the midst of an unparalleled expenditure, began to decline on the
re-establishment of tranquillity, and of at least
a comparative economy. While innumerable
obstacles were thrown in the way of her trade,
she burst them all, and supplied the commercial wants of the world. When those obstacles
were in a great measure removed, her efforts seemed on a sudden to be paralized. The causes of
this anomaly I have already endeavoured to
trace: even if I have been unsuccessful, we
must search for them in some other quarter

than in our own profuse expenditure during
the war, which never, in any possible circumstances, can be the parent of even a temporary
semblance of national prosperity.

SECTION IV.

EFFECTS OF THE TAXES IMPOSED DURING THE WAR.

The immense load of taxes imposed on Britain during the war was unable to repress the
industry of the country, stimulated as it was by
an extensive and increasing demand for every
commodity that our farmers or manufacturers
could produce. Every one knew that he
would have been richer had not those taxes
been imposed; but finding himself able, from
year to year, either to improve his style of living, or to add to his capital, he submitted with

patience to what was only a privation of pos-sible gratifications, especially as he might have some doubts whether the war, by which this ne-cessity was created, might not be a principal cause of his prosperity.

But taxes, which during this state of things had been disregarded, became oppressive, when the sources of our income were in some degree dried up. That which had been paid without difficulty, and which seemed merely to check the progress of luxury in its rapid advance, now bore hard on the comforts, and even on the ne-cessaries, of life; and, by preventing accumula-tion on the one hand, and decreasing popula-tion on the other, seemed to lead, by easy and almost unavoidable steps, to national impove-rishment.

To this cause, accordingly, the late distresses of the country seem to have been most gene-rally ascribed; and serious doubts have been en-tertained by many, whether the country, during peace, could continue to pay the interest of the national debt. Such doubts have perhaps prevailed more generally abroad than at home, and even Mr Say seems to have adopted them to a very considerable extent *.

In order to form a just estimate of the degree in which the taxes contribute to the distress that has been so generally felt in this country, it will be necessary to review, in succession, their influence on the condition of some of the principal classes into which the population is naturally divided.

At a time when, from other causes, the wages of labour are depressed, every tax, such as the cottage tax, which is directly levied from the poor, and every duty which, by raising the price of the necessaries or comforts enjoyed by the lower orders, affects them indirectly, must great-

---

* Lettres à M. Malthus.—Lettre 3 me.

ly aggravate the public distress.   While wages were high, a rise in the price of his shoes, salt, beer, soap, candles, tea, sugar, tobacco, and a few other articles of his expense, though it limited his enjoyments, left to a workman many of the comforts, and all the necessaries, of life. From year to year his condition was rather improving ; and he was scarcely aware how much faster it might have improved, had no taxes on the articles of his daily consumption been imposed.   But when his wages were reduced to that which, even without taxation, could scarcely have maintained his family, each little sum, indirectly withdrawn from his revenue to swell that of the state, brought him nearer to that deplorable condition, in which, from a slight accident, or a farther decline in the demand for labour, he might be forced to endure the utmost extremity of want.   It was in such circumstances that the Minister of Britain, in 1819, proposed, and the Parliament sanctioned, the imposition of three millions of annual taxes, all of which, in proportion to their respective incomes, fell much heavier on the poor than on the rich *.

That such taxes add greatly to the misery produced by other causes, there cannot be a doubt; and to all other miseries they add that of public discontent. From a workman reduced from comparative affluence to nearly bare subsistence, part of his remaining pittance is wrested by Government; and it is impossible that he should not deeply feel how materially this sum, small as it is, would have contributed to the comfort, perhaps to the health, of his family. His impoverishment has been the result of public measures over which he had no control; and the hand of Government, in place

---

* The articles selected for taxation were malt, tea, tobacco, English spirits, and foreign wool which is used, I believe, for the coarser cloths.

of being stretched out for his relief, crushes him more completely to the earth.

It was in vain that emigration was facilitated to those who were incapacitated, partly by taxation, from subsisting at home. The most destitute were unable to avail themselves of the offers of Government; nor, in their circumstances, depressed, friendless, destitute, and many of them unused to country labour, could they, with any reasonable prospect of bettering their condition, have encountered the hardships of a new settlement in a distant and unknown region. The number also of those, for whom the means of emigration were provided, was much too limited to produce the slightest amendment on the condition of such as remained behind. But had it been otherwise, it was very questionable policy to seek an escape from present evil, by means which, if effectual for the immediate object, must have cramped the future prosperity of the country. That in proportion to our capital there was no excess of population, seemed almost certain, from the full employment, at high wages, which that capital had lately been able to supply to the people. The capital still remained, but the demand for the produce both of the capital and labour had declined. In such circumstances, the cheapness of our goods, joined to the increasing wealth of other nations, afforded the chief hope of such an increase of demand as would again give full employment both to our capital and our workmen. Had we succeeded in thinning our population, wages would indeed have advanced for a time; but if the prices of our goods advanced along with them, our manufactures would have been less able to force themselves into the foreign market; and if their prices did not advance, profits would have been so depressed that our capital could not have been retained in the country. In either case, our workmen, after a short season of relief, would again have found themselves without employment, and an extensive emigration, without being productive of

permanent good, would immediately have reduced the power and wealth of the nation, and
ultimately shut out every prospect of returning
prosperity *.

The effect of a repeal of all those taxes that
press upon the lower orders would, however, be
neither trivial nor temporary. By such a measure, the comforts of the people would at once
be increased, without any diminution of their
numbers, or rise in the wages of labour; the
cheapness of our productions, without either
wearing down our capital by commercial losses,
or driving it from the country by want of
profitable employment, would force our goods

* I trust I shall not be suspected of recommending that
any obstacles should be thrown in the way of emigration,
though I doubt the policy of holding out direct encouragement
to it. To prevent any man from leaving the country, whenever he may wish to do so, is contrary to every principle of
liberty ; and I have always viewed the imbecile, unjust, and oppressive laws against the emigration of mechanics as a disgrace
to the Statute Book.

into every corner of the world; and the increase
of demand, as the nations around us formed
a taste for our manufactures, or advanced in
wealth, would pave the way to a future rise of
wages, from which no evil could result. The
relief would be immediate, the benefits permanent and progressive.

The effect of the taxation of commodities,
either when imported or manufactured, as already explained, is to raise the price of such
commodities, and thereby to discourage their
consumption. By raising the price of our productions, taxes of this description would have
a direct tendency to restrict their sale abroad,
and sometimes to exclude them entirely from
foreign markets, were not this prevented by
drawbacks or bounties equal to the duty
imposed on the importation of the raw produce, and in a few instances also to the
taxes levied on the manufacture. To those
drawbacks there does not seem to be any objection on principle, though in practice they some-

times afford means of defrauding the revenue.
They merely allow our goods to enter the great
market of Europe, on the same footing with
those from countries less loaded with public
debt, and thus replace them in the situation
which they would have held, had no such
duties been imposed. To make foreigners pay
any part of our taxes, besides being unjust, is
always a chimerical attempt. Our goods, at
all times, sell abroad for the highest price
obtainable in the foreign market ; and as this
price depends partly on the demand, partly on
the competition of foreign commodities, it cannot be raised, without either diminishing the
general consumption of the article, or transferring the supply of it to some other country.

By drawbacks the foreign market may be
retained ; but as there can be no drawback
for the inconvenience and vexation arising
from fiscal regulations, some tax is still imposed on those who prepare goods for the foreign
market ; and the rise of price in the home mar-

ket consequent on taxation, by diminishing consumption, narrows very considerably the employment both of capital and industry. This is unavoidable; for, the public debt having been contracted, there is probably no way of paying its interest, less objectionable than by those taxes on commodities which fall ultimately on the consu mer. But it is not on that account the less true, that the diminution of the consumption of taxed articles, by contracting the employment of capital, lowers the ordinary rate of profit, and, along with those other circumstances by which profits have also been lowered, will tend, though probably in no very material degree, to induce the removal of our capital to other countries.

It is also so obvious as to require merely to be stated, that the reduction of profits, which is a consequence of taxation, diminishes that fund, and discourages that economy, from which the annual accumulation of capital must be derived; an evil which, though unavoidable, must not be overlooked in reviewing the present state, and estimating the future prospects, of the country.

Since the repeal of the property tax, no part of the public revenue, with the exception of a few taxes unfavourable to agriculture, seems to press with undue severity on the landed interest. The same income will undoubtedly command fewer of the comforts or luxuries of life, after their price is raised by taxation; but I have already stated the grounds on which I believe that rents, though much reduced in their money rates, and perhaps in reality not quite so high by the acre as during the latter period of the war, are higher in the aggregate than they would have been under an uninterrupted peace. The demand for the produce of land induced the farmers to cultivate more, and to cultivate better; and in the amelioration of their estates, landholders have a fund from which they can pay the advanced prices of all the articles which they consume.   If there be any doubt on this subject, it must arise from the enormous increase of poor's rates, which, in many parts of England, has been the consequence of the depressed condition of labourers and mechanics*.

Upon the whole, if the taxes have enormously increased, the funds from which those taxes are drawn, independently of the present depression which is probably of a temporary nature, seem also to have been much augmented.   That every one would be more comfortable if he had fewer taxes to pay, is undoubted; but in the general affluence of the country, as evinced by the indulgences, luxuries, splendour and magnificence, of the middling and higher ranks of society, there seem a sufficient guarantee to the public creditor, and sufficient sources of public revenue, without decreasing the national wealth.   In

---

* It is almost unnecessary to remark, that poor's rates, whether paid in the first instance by landlord or tenant, are ultimately a charge upon the rent.

such circumstances, there can be no apology, as there is no necessity, for any breach of contract with the national creditors. All that can be required, on the most unfavourable supposi-tions, is, that the higher ranks of society, who at present indulge in show and luxuries, which, though very expensive, are little conducive to their real happiness, should abate somewhat of their magnificence, and dedicate the fruits of their self-denial to the preservation of the public faith. Nor does it seem unreasonable to demand such a sacrifice from those who, to the very last, strenuously supported that war, by which the public debt has been entailed upon the nation. These considerations, however, can form no apology for the slightest depar-ture from rigid economy. Every sixpence unnecessarily levied from the people is both an injustice and oppression; an injustice, as it de-prives some person of his property without an equivalent; and an oppression, by multiplying those restraints on liberty, without which a very large revenue can scarcely be levied.

Now that the public debt has been contracted, all that Government can do, besides prac-
tising the most rigid economy, is to repeal the
taxes on such articles as are used by the poor ;
and if the public revenue be thus rendered deficient, to increase those that fall exclusively on
the rich. If by these means our population
can be maintained, without emigration, on the
low wages to which, by the circumstances of the
country, they have been reduced, the diminution
of the poor's rates, the increased demand for
the produce of the land, and the revived commerce of the country, will more than compensate to the higher orders the privations to
which, for some time, they may be obliged to
submit.

There is one danger, however, attending this
proceeding, which, though not very formidable,
it would be improper to overlook. The great
expense of living in Britain, compared to that
on the Continent, has already induced many
families to go abroad, and to spend those in-

comes in the encouragement of foreign industry, which, if they had remained at home, would have supplied a market for our own productions. Were the rich to be still farther taxed, either directly, or through a rise in the price of living, in order that the taxes now affecting the poor might be repealed, it may be feared that so many might follow the example which has been set them, that wages would be still farther lowered, and the condition of the people, in place of being improved, would be injured.

Of these consequences I confess I am not very apprehensive. Mere cheapness of living will not tempt many to abandon their country and their friends, to change all their tastes and habits, and to throw themselves for life among strangers in whom they feel no interest, and from whom they have nothing to expect but the common offices of civility. Indeed there are few cases in which expatriation is likely to be attended with even pecuniary advantages.

The landholder would lose more by commit-
ting the management of his estate to an
attorney, than he could save in the price of the
articles consumed in his family: the merchant
would be unwilling either to leave his trade to
clerks whom he could not superintend, or to
remove his establishments to a country with
whose wants, manner of transacting business,
and mercantile regulations, he was imperfectly
acquainted: even the capitalist, unless tempted
by very high interest rather than by cheapness
of living, will prefer lending his money where he
has the best means of information regarding his
debtors, the greatest dependence on their
punctuality, and the most entire confidence in
the administration of law; and as his own
country will in these respects, even from habit,
obtain his preference, he will lend his money at
home, and reside where he can easiest watch
over the nature of its investment. Although,
therefore, some may go abroad for the purpose
of retrenchment, they will neither be so many,
nor so opulent, that the loss of their expenditure

can perceptibly affect the demand for our raw produce or manufactures.

By those who consider taxation as the chief bar to our prosperity, it has been proposed to pay off the national debt by one or a few great contributions, and thus to reduce the public revenue to the sum required for the current expenses of the year. By so doing, there seems no doubt that we should in a great degree get rid of the heavy salaries and poundages allowed to the numerous officers by whom the public revenue is collected and managed, and also that we should be able at once to abolish all taxes which bear hard on the lower orders, or shackle any branch of our commerce or manufactures. These advantages are indisputable; but important as they are, they may be bought too dear.

The attempt to make personal property contribute towards the extinction of the national debt, would have an effect very different from

that of the high price of living, in inducing capitalists to emigrate and carry their wealth to
other countries.   He who never would have
thought of quitting his friends and country, to
live more cheaply or more luxuriously among
strangers, would readily go abroad for a few
years, if by so doing he could save a considerable portion of his wealth from legal seizure;
and after having left his country for this purpose, formed new connections, and vested his
money abroad, he might not always return,
when the cause of his expatriation had ceased.
By this emigration of capital, even our workmen would probably lose much more, in want of
demand for their labour, and consequent reduction of wages, than they could gain by exemption from the taxes which they now pay; while
the wealth, prosperity, and power of the nation,
would be materially, perhaps irretrievably, injured.

The exportation of wealth, the devices that

would be fallen upon to conceal that which remained, and the impossibility of ascertaining
the amount of mercantile stock even under very
inquisitorial proceedings, would, in opposition
to every principle of justice, throw the repay-
ment of the public debt almost entirely on
the landholders. This injustice could not even
be measured by the heavy contributions to
which they would be subjected ; for either they
would have to borrow money at an enormous
interest, in the vain hope of paying off the in-
cumbrance by extreme parsimony, or they would
be forced to sell their lands at a very depreciated value. Having no other means of paying their contributions, it is plain that they
must either borrow or sell. But partly from
the exportation of capital, still more from the
determination of the capitalists that remained in the country to keep the command of
their funds, that they might avail themselves of
those favourable occurrences which could not
fail to arise, it would be almost impossible to do

the one, and almost ruinous to do the other. The landholders would be forced to have their contributions ready at a fixed time, under heavy penalties and law expenses; those who possessed circulating capital might either lend it for a time on merchants' bills, or make temporary purchases in foreign funds, or even keep it by them unemployed, certain that the accumulating distresses of landholders would speedily, in one way or other, enable them to realise extravagant profits. Thus would one class of the community be plundered, not only directly by the state, but also indirectly by their creditors, or by the purchasers of their lands.

Nor would the mercantile classes escape without losses more than equivalent to the taxes from which they were ultimately to be relieved. Every sum of money which they had borrowed would be demanded from them, that it might be ready to be lent out at an interest which no commercial speculation could bear, or to be vested in lands, which, by the distress of the land-holders, were forced upon the market. It is true, that when the operation of discharging the national debt was completed, the whole capital that had been thus called up, with the exception of that which had been sent abroad, would again be returned to its former investments; the capital set free from the public funds being precisely equal to that by which the public debt was extinguished. But in the mean time, mercantile speculations would have been deranged; machinery, from want of circulating capital, would have been thrown idle; and bankruptcy, beginning with those who traded extensively on borrowed money, would have gradually spread even to the wealthy and the prudent.

Without, therefore, being of opinion, that the slightest advantage of any kind is derived from the national debt, I see no means, consistent with justice and sound policy, by which that debt can be reduced, except an ample and effective sinking fund during peace*. This

---

* Dr Hamilton, in his very luminous Inquiry concerning the national debt, has so fully exposed the quackery of a pretended sinking fund during war, while the total amount of the debt is annually increased, that even during peace the sinking fund seems in danger of falling into disrepute. This extension, however, of Dr Hamilton's censure, proceeds entirely on a misapprehension of his reasonings, all of which support the opposite conclusion. With regard to the effect of a sinking fund on national wealth, I beg to refer to the Elements of Political Science, Book III. Part. iii. chap. 3.

No proposition, indeed, can be more demonstrable, than that a regular increase of the national debt during every war, without a corresponding decrease during peace, must lead to national bankruptcy. The time may be indefinite; but the result is certain.

It would be well if those who have derived all their opinions on this subject from Dr Hamilton's book (and they could not have drawn them from a purer source), would read that book with more attention, and own with greater fairness their obligations to its author. For although constant reference to authorities would be tedious in an oration, our senators (not one of whom, I believe, has yet named Dr Hamilton in either House of Parliament) should remember that plagiarism is not less reprehensible in a spoken, than in a written, discourse.

sinking fund may be derived either from public, or from private, parsimony. That the first might be rendered adequate both for this purpose, and for the relief of the lower orders from the taxes by which they are oppressed, it might be rash to assert : but when we contrast the present peace establishment with that which followed the American war, and recollect that of all the public officers whose allowances were increased during the depreciation of the currency, scarcely one has been reduced to his former salary since that apology ceased to exist; when we farther throw our eye over the long list of offices which are either acknowledged sinecures, or of which the greater part of the duties are devolved on substitutes, it is impossible to doubt that, by public economy, much might be done towards the gradual extinction of the national debt. Should this, however, be insufficient, taxes must be levied, by which private economy, not indeed without occasioning serious hardships to some classes of the people, must be brought in aid of that of the state; and all that can be wished in such circumstances is, that the taxes may be so imposed, as to fall on the rich, without distressing the poor, or discouraging that industry on which the future wealth and power of the nation immediately depend.

A very different view of the effects of public expenditure on national wealth, and consequently of the duties of Government in respect to the employment and salaries of public officers, is often heard in the conversation of ignorant persons, and has even been pompously set forth in some recent publications. Ascribing very justly our prosperity, during the late war, to the unexampled demand for our goods, it has been seriously proposed to keep up this demand during peace, by the continuance of a large and expensive establishment, by the erection of magnificent public works ; and, in short, by increasing, rather than contracting, the public expenditure,

To examine in detail so extravagant a proposal, would be a waste of time; but it may be shortly remarked, that all public revenue must be drawn either from private revenue or from capital; if from the former, the decrease of the demand by individuals will exactly correspond to its increase occasioned by the public expenditure; if from the latter, the nation will be impoverished from year to year, and, exactly in the same proportion, will the home demand for articles of consumption annually decline.

FINIS.